The Bonhoeffer Legacy:
An International Journal

The Bonhoeffer Legacy: An International Journal
Volume 8, Issue 1 2020

The Bonhoeffer Legacy: An International Journal is a fully refereed academic journal aimed principally at providing an outlet for an ever expanding Bonhoeffer scholarship in Australia, New Zealand and the South Pacific region, as well as being open to article submissions from Bonhoeffer scholars throughout the world. It also aims to elicit and encourage future and ongoing scholarship in the field. The focus of the journal, captured in the notion of 'Legacy', is on any aspect of Bonhoeffer's life, theology and political action that is relevant to his immense contribution to twentieth century events and scholarship. 'Legacy' can be understood as including those events and ideas that contributed to Bonhoeffer's own development, those that constituted his own context or those that have developed since his time as a result of his work. The editors encourage and welcome any scholarship that contributes to the journal's aims. The journal also has book reviews.

Business Manager
Mr Hilary Regan, Publisher, ATF Theology, PO Box 504 Hindmarsh, SA 5007, Australia.
Fax +61 8 82235643.

Subscription Rates

Print	On-line	Print and On-line
Aus $65 Individuals	Aus $55 individuals	Aus $75 individuals
Aus $90 Institutions	Aus $80 individuals	Aus $100 instiutions

The Bonhoeffer Legacy: An International Journal is published by ATF Theology an imprint of ATF (Australia) Ltd (ABN 90 116 359 963) and is published once a year.
ISSN 2202-9168

ISBN:	978-1-922737-17-5	soft
	978-1-922737-18-2	hard
	978-1-922737-19-9	epub
	978-1-922737-20-5	pdf

This periodical is indexed in the ATLA Religion Database® (ATLA RDB®), a product of the American Theological Library Association.
Email: atla@atla.com<mailto:atla@atla.com>, www: http://www.atla.com<http://www.atla.com/>.

THEOLOGY

The Bonhoeffer Legacy:
An International Journal

THEOLOGY
2020

Vol 8 No 1/2020

Contents

Bibliography

The Dietrich Bonhoeffer Works (English)

General Editors: Victoria Barnett, Wayne Whitson Floyd Jr., and Barbara Wojhoski.

Originally published in German as *Dietrich Bonhoeffer Werke*. Edited by Eberhard Bethge et al. Munich: Chr. Kaiser Verlag, 1986–1998.

DBWE 1   *Sanctorum Communio: A Theological Study of the Sociology of the Church*. Edited by Clifford J. Green. Translated by Reinhard Krauss and Nancy Lukens. Minneapolis: Fortress, 1998.

DBWE 2   *Act and Being: Transcendental Philosophy and Ontology in Systematic Theology*. Edited by Wayne Whitson Floyd, Jr. Translated by H. Martin Rumscheidt. Minneapolis: Fortress, 1998.

DBWE 3   *Creation and Fall: A Theological Exposition of Genesis 1–3*. Edited by John W. de Gruchy. Translated by Douglas Stephen Bax. Minneapolis: Fortress, 1997.

DBWE 4   *Discipleship*. Edited by Geffrey B. Kelly and John D. Godsey. Translated by Barbara Green and Reinhard Krauss. Minneapolis: Fortress, 2001.

DBWE 5   *Life Together; Prayerbook of the Bible*. Edited by Geffrey B. Kelly. Translated by Daniel W. Bloesch and James H. Burtness. Minneapolis: Fortress, 1996.

DBWE 6   *Ethics*. Edited by Clifford J. Green. Translated by Reinhard Krauss, Charles C. West and Douglas W. Stott. Minneapolis: Fortress, 2005.

DBWE 7   *Fiction from Tegel Prison.* Edited by Clifford Green. Translated by Nancy Lukens. Minneapolis: Fortress, 2000.

DBWE 8   *Letters and Papers from Prison.* Edited by John de Gruchy. Translated by Reinhard Krauss and Nancy Lukens.Minneapolis: Fortress, 2010.

DBWE 9   *The Young Bonhoeffer: 1918–1927.* Edited by Paul Duane Matheny, Clifford J. Green and Marshall D. Johnson. Translated by Mary C. Nebelsick and Douglas W. Stott. Minneapolis: Fortress, 2002.

DBWE 10   *Barcelona, Berlin, New York.* Edited by Clifford J. Green. Translated by Douglas W. Stott. Minneapolis: Fortress, 2008.

DBWE 11   *Ecumenical, Academic, and Pastoral Work: 1931–1932.* Edited by Victoria J. Barnett, Mark S. Brocker and Michael B. Lukens. Translated by Anne Schmidt-Lange, Isabel Best, Nicolas Humphrey, Marion Pauck and Douglas W. Stott. Minneapolis: Fortress, 2012.

DBWE 12   *Berlin: 1932–1933.* Edited by Larry L. Rasmussen. Translated by Isabel Best. Minneapolis: Fortress, 2009.

DBWE 13   *London: 1933–1935.* Edited by Keith W. Clements. Translated by Isabel Best. Minneapolis: Fortress, 2007.

DBWE 14   *Theological Education Finkenwalde: 1935–1937.* Edited by Victoria J. Barnett. Translated by Peter Frick. Minneapolis: Fortress, 2011.

DBWE 15   *Theological Education Underground: 1937–1940.* Edited by Victoria J. Barnett. Translated by Claudia D. Bergmann and Peter Frick. Minneapolis: Fortress, 2011.

DBWE 16   *Conspiracy and Imprisonment: 1940–1945.* Edited by Mark S. Brocker. Translated by Lisa E. Dahill. Minneapolis: Fortress, 2006.

DBWE 17   *Indexes and Supplementary Materials.* Edited by Victoria J. Barnett and Barbara Wojhoski. Minneapolis: Fortress, 2014.

Vol 8 No 1/2020

Editorial

The Bonhoeffer Legacy: An International Journal, now in its eighth volume, was initiated principally to provide an outlet for an ever-expanding Bonhoeffer scholarship in Australia, New Zealand, and the South Pacific region, one that has included an annual conference since 2004 and a range of symposia and other events called from time to time by Bonhoeffer scholars and interested parties. The initial aim was to support and encourage this extant scholarship from the Australasian region as well as to forge links with and draw into the region the wider and ever-expanding Bonhoeffer scholarship to be found internationally. The international links have grown significantly during the past eight years, indicated by an increasing authorship in and subscriptions to the journal coming from all parts of the world. As a result, the Editorial Board made the decision a year ago to re-name the journal slightly, with a new sub-title, *An International Journal*, that captures this reality.

The focus of the journal, seen in the notion of 'Legacy', remains on any aspect of Bonhoeffer's life, theology and/or political action that is relevant to his immense contribution to twentieth and twenty-first century events and scholarship. 'Legacy' can be understood to include those events and ideas that contributed to Bonhoeffer's own development, those that constituted his own context or those that have developed since his time as a result of his work and the many commentaries on it. In other words, Bonhoeffer's legacy can be traced back to the events, philosophies and theologies that preceded his time as well as drawn forward to help in understanding the world we inhabit today, especially around issues of faith, non-faith and the ethics entailed in human action.

This first issue of the eighth volume is presented in honour of Professor John Moses. Now well into his nineties, Professor Moses has been a giant figure in Australian Bonhoeffer studies, a regular keynote presenter and attendant at Australian Bonhoeffer conferences and a regular participant at international Bonhoeffer gatherings. His distinctive work that melds Bonhoeffer's theology with the political context of his work is featured in the lead article, titled, *Surveying Bonhoeffer's Spiritual Pilgrimage*. The article amplifies the change of heart and mind that Bonhoeffer underwent in moving from his early formation in Prusso-German thinking and assumptions to taking the path of resistance to the Third Reich that characterises his academic work and practical action. The point is that it was from his belief in and understanding of God revealed in Christ that Bonhoeffer was able to displace his cultural intuitions. Peter Hooton offers an article that, without any intention, can be seen as building on this theme. The article, *Breaking the Circle of the Self: Bonhoeffer and the Religious a Priori,* grapples with Bonhoeffer's challenge of the notion that religious belief emanates from a deep-seated religious intuition. For Bonhoeffer, it is clear that the beliefs that drove his actions, deemed radical by many, came from God's revelation of self through Christ.

The third article by Joel Looper, *Reading the Luther Bible with Dietrich Bonhoeffer*, is again not unrelated to the theme already established. Looper argues that key parts of Bonhoeffer's work can remain a little indiscernible if the Luther Bible is not a constant reading companion. Included in examples is one where Bonhoeffer refers to Hitler as 'anti-Christ', so setting him against his own cultural formation on the basis of his understanding of the God revealed in Christ. The fourth article by Myles Werntz, *Bearing the Impossible Present: Bonhoeffer, Illegality and the Witness for Migrants*, employs a lecture Bonhoeffer gave to ordinands for wisdom as to how to negotiate the space and tension between contemporary law surrounding immigration and future aspirations regarding the law. He uses the example of the US's current struggle with the issue of immigration as a case study.

Finally, this issue offers two book reviews. First, John Moses reviews his fellow nonagenarian, John Shelby Spong's recent book, *Biblical Literalism: A Gentile Heresy: A Journey into a New Christianity through the Doorway of Matthew's Gospel,* as one that profoundly challenges populist fundamentalism, with reference to Bonhoeffer's own positioning on biblical literalism. It was while this issue was being prepared that we heard of the death of Bishop Spong. The review therefore serves to honour his remarkable contribution to Christian theology, as well as being further testimony to the wide-ranging and often innovative contribution that Professor Moses has made to Bonhoeffer studies. In the second review, Terence Lovat reviews *Dietrich Bonhoeffer, Theology, and Political Resistance* by Lori Brandt Hale and W David Hall. Among other things, the central theme of the book fits well with the undercurrent of Bonhoeffer's political theology that runs through this issue of *The Bonhoeffer Legacy*.

As we continue to suggest, Bonhoeffer's theology is akin to the unfinished symphony and so possesses an unusual capacity to be taken in any number of directions and to continue to stimulate new theological, ethical, and indeed political thought. The Bonhoeffer legacy is unusual in its capacity to take us back to some of the most ancient of theological considerations as well as sharpen our attention to issues alive at the present time.

Terence Lovat
The University of Newcastle, Australia
September 2021

Surveying Bonhoeffer's Spiritual Journey

John A Moses

Introduction

In my book, *Reluctant Revolutionary . . .*,[1] I portrayed Bonhoeffer's spiritual journey as a harrowing learning experience in which an essentially conservative but humane person learned how to critique the Nazi regime by rigorously applying his theological training but from within the political culture of Bismarckian-Wilhelmine Germany in which he was educated. It was not as though at any stage the young Bonhoeffer had become an Anglo-Saxon Whig who would endorse a political revolution in order to bring about a just society. Rather, Bonhoeffer offers an example of a rigorously Christian *Bildungsbürger* who could think through the implications of that inherited mind-set during a time of existential crisis. *Bildungsbürger* of that stamp were people of a highly educated and cultured class of Germans, representing a unique phenomenon in the Western world. They were quite distinctive from the middle classes in the Anglo-sphere or other European countries.

Bildungsbürgertum

In retrospect, the so-called *Bildungsbürgertum*, which may be translated as the *educated German bourgeoisie*, presents as a positive cul-

*I am indebted to Dr Ilse Tödt of Heidelberg for her constructive criticism of an earlier draft of this paper prepared for the annual *Bonhoeffer Conference* held at Kincumber NSW 31ˢᵗ July-1ˢᵗ August 2014.

1. *Reluctant Revolutionary: Dietrich Bonhoeffer's Collision with Prusso-German History* 2ⁿᵈ edition (New York: Berghahn Books, 2013).

tural phenomenon, at least in normal times, but as a potential liability in times of political crisis. This is partly because its members did not perceive themselves as pro-actively political in any way. Hence, in their uncritical submissiveness to the powers-that-be, they failed to develop what Anglo-Saxons might call a 'whiggish' attitude to State power, summed up arguably in the English concept of 'loyal opposition', seen best in the peculiarly English 'Whig tradition'.[2] The German *bourgeoisie*, by and large, never developed that concept or took it to its logical constitutional conclusion.

It might be considered one of the great historical tragedies of our time that the German *bourgeoisie*, with few exceptions, never aspired to political leadership to the same degree as did their equivalent numbers in the Western European and trans-Atlantic community of nations. Explaining why this was so has occupied the attention of many German historians and sociologists to the present day.[3] This is especially dramatic when it is appreciated that the world's largest and best organised modern democratic party and labour organisations, such as the Social Democratic Party and its allied trade unions,[4] had developed in Germany from 1848 through to 1918. They suffered however from perennial legal marginalisation despite the Social Democratic Party, prior to the First World War, rising to become the largest single party in the *Reichstag*.[5]

This paper addresses the question concerning how the monarchical, bureaucratic, and indeed militaristic political culture rose in Prusso-Germany to determine the nature of politics. In doing so, one needs to be aware of the peculiar nature of Church-State relations in Germany from the time of the Reformation. What has to be grasped is the extent to which the alleged spiritual character of the State in Protestant German thinking impinged on the mental, political and

---

2. For people who do not like the term 'Anglo-Saxon' perhaps the expression 'trans-Atlantic community' might be preferable. In German, however, the term *die Angelsachsen* is current in German usage to refer to all the successor states to the British Empire, that is the USA, Canada, Australia, and New Zealand.

3. See the multi-volume work entitled, *Bildungsbügertum im 19. Jahrhundert* 4 volumes edited by Werner Conze and Jürgen Kocka (Stuttgart: Klett Kotta, 1985–1989).

4. John A Moses, *Trade Unionism in Germany from Bismarck to Hitler 1862–1933*, 2 volumesa (London/New York: George Prior/ Barnes & Noble, 1980).

5. This is explained at length in my book referenced in the previous footnote.

cultural formation of the common people, rather than merely on the *Bildungsbürgertum*. This is essential background to comprehending the career of Pastor Dr Dietrich Bonhoeffer whose memory today is honoured throughout the world. It is hoped that the following excursus will shed light on the circumstances that moulded the young Bonhoeffer into becoming a 'reluctant revolutionary'. It was a spiritual as much as an intellectual journey.

The Crucial Prussian Hegemony

A major factor in German history that is often overlooked is the extent to which the Kingdom of Prussia came to exert hegemonic influence over the development of German political culture. It displaced the relatively long liberal tradition that had once prevailed in the south-west kingdoms of Baden and Württemberg, as well as in the Rhineland and the Hanseatic city states. Their liberal tradition was unable to outweigh the influence of Prussia that, by the time of unification in 1870–1871, was the largest German principality by far, a kingdom with a population larger than France. It was further distinguished by the fact that it was essentially a military monarchy, meaning that the State was organised by its bureaucracy to maintain and enhance the efficiency of the army. Commenting on this fact, the notable south-German liberal Roman Catholic historian Franz Schnabel (1887–1966) memorably observed that Prussia was like one great military barracks where everyone in his or her professional capacity (*Beruf*) in some way served the needs of the army.[6] Importantly, there was no shortage of educators who, well before Bismarck's successful unification of Germany, prophesied that it was Prussia's vocation under Almighty God to unify the other Germanic states under her political culture.[7]

---

6. Franz Schnabel, *Deutsche Geschichte im 19. Jahrhundert*, 4 volumes (Freiburg: Herder Verlag), I: 95–97
7. For information on how 19th century German historians exercised a powerful educative influence on nationalism, especially in teaching that it was Prussia's vocation throughout history to unite Germany under her particular military culture, see George, G Iggers, *The German Conception of History: The National Tradition of Historical Thought from Herder to the Present* (Middletown, Conn: Wesleyan University Press, 1968).

The spiritual father of these historical propagandists was the son of an army chaplain from Treptow on the Rega in Pomerania, namely, Johann Gustav Droysen (1808–1884). After the failure of the 1848 revolutions in Germany to bring effect to a national government, Droysen produced a multi-volume work titled, *Die Geschichte der preussischen Politik* (5 volumes, 1855–1886). In this work, he developed the doctrine of *Borussismus*. The doctrine proposed that from the foundation of the electorate of Brandenburg under the Hohenzollerns, namely, the region around Berlin, Almighty God had pre-ordained that it should expand throughout the course of history and eventually unite all the other Germanic principalities.

Droysen, trained as a Hellenist, depicted Prussia as the 'Sparta of the North'. This idea is contained in the notion that the military kingdom of Sparta in ancient Greece provided a historical model for modern Prussia. The notion constituted a remarkably influential historical pedagogy, influencing many of its pupils, including Heinrich von Treitschke (1834–1896) who, at the peak of his career, rejoiced in the appellation of 'The Bismarck of the Professorial Chair'.[8] In turn, von Treitschke's influence on the political education of the German *bourgeoisie* was enduring and all-pervading. Far from a salutary influence, he became the virulent prophet of both Prusso-German military expansion and its inherent anti-Semitism. To him was attributed the formula, "The Jews are our misfortune" which Adolf Hitler and his followers utilised. Julius Streicher, in his Nazi propaganda newspaper, *Der Stürmer*, repeated the phrase *ad nauseam*.[9] The intellectual link between von Treitschke and Streicher is undeniable. Furthermore, while in Landsberg prison in 1924, Hitler read voraciously the works of von Treitschke, as well as von Ranke, which no doubt influenced the values that would eventually characterise his legacy.[10]

---

8. Heinrich Ritter von Srbik, *Geist und Geschichte vom Deutschem Humanismus bis zur Gegenwart*, 2 volumes (Munich: Bruckmann Verlag, 1964). On page 386 of volume I Srbik describes Treitschke as the 'priest and prophet' of the German national power state (*Machtstaat*). His further portrayal of Treitschke is virtually an indictment of his role in championing the 'Prussianisation' of Germany (385–398) which from an Austrian point of view was justified. See also, Andreas Dorpalen, 'Heinrich von Treitschke' *in Journal of Contemporary History*, volume 7, 3/4 (October 1972): 21–35.

9. Treitschke first used the phrase "The Jews are our misfortune" in the journal *Die preussischen Jahrbücher* in 1879.

10. Eberhard Jäckel, *Hitler's Weltanschauung: a Blueprint for Power* (Middletown Conn: Wesleyan University Press, 1972).

The Powers-that-be are Ordained of God

One needs to recall that Dietrich Bonhoeffer was a product of a Prussian education system from prior to the Great War. He would have been conditioned to perceive the State as the *Obrigkeit,* meaning the "powers-that-be ordained by God", as recorded in St Paul's Epistle to the Romans, chapter XIII. Notably, Professor Walther-Peter Fuchs (1904–1997), a leading Reformation historian at the University of Erlangen, designated Romans XIII as arguably the most important document in German history.[11] Why? Because the Lutheran Church in Germany had, since the Reformation, perceived the prince as the *Obrigkeit.* The absolutist prince (*Landesfürst*) had replaced the Pope as *summus episcopus,* so he was not only a monarch by divine right but also the head of the church. The Protestant prince in Germany became both Head of State and Head of Church in subtly different ways from those roles as they evolved in post-Reformation Britain. Within the Germanic states, the two roles were merged with the result that Church and State became effectively the one entity, a historically unique development. This phenomenon affected Prusso-German political culture down to Bonhoeffer's time, having led to the emergence of a concept of service that saw service to the State as an essential element in the 'economy of God'. *Gottesdienst,* Lutheran worship, was an expression of faithfulness to both Church and State. Part of the notion had it that in carrying out one's daily work, whether it be on the farm or in the factory, in the public service or the army, whether one was the hangman or the pastor, all were components that combined organically to function as the 'economy of God' for the general good, that which preserved 'civil society'.

---

11. As a member of Professor Fuch's *Oberseminar* at the University of Erlangen in 1963 I participated in the investigation of the influence of Luther and Calvin on German and Austrian historians over 100 years, starting with Leopold von Ranke in the mid-19th century and ending with Gerhard Ritter mid 20th century writing. The overwhelming majority of history professors and teachers in secondary schools in Germany were so-called 'statists' following Ranke's Lutheran-influenced understanding of the role of state authority in history (*Romans* XIII) and then with the rise of the 'Prussian' school most became advocates of a form of determinism. That meant they believed, following Gustav von Droysen, (see above. following footnote 7) that they could affirm a calling by Prussia to unite Germany under its hegemony. The efficacy of their teaching is bourne out by the catastrophic course of German history.

The point is that everybody in the nation/kingdom, in whatever capacity or calling, was serving the community, and so by definition, also serving God. The notion was reinforced by Luther himself in that the world was conceived as the 'Devil's Inn', or public house, *des Teufels Wirtshaus* in which good, law abiding and pious subjects who ventured therein for refreshment and lodging were exposed to all manner of threats, deception, and temptation. The 'Devil's Inn' was a metaphor for the world. There was therefore an obvious need for the strong arm of the State, as God's police force, to maintain law and order so that peaceful subjects might fulfil their respective callings unmolested. The 'economy of God' had to be protected. Hence, a central authority under God was essential and this was given expression through a strong police force, a strong judiciary, a strong bureaucracy and, above all, a strong army to preserve the kingdom from the incursions and depredations of envious foreign powers. In this way, Machiavellianism triumphed in Prusso-Germany, as leading scholars, such as Friedrich Meinecke, have demonstrated.[12]

The consequence of all the above was that Prussia developed into a highly authoritarian state. In 1871, with the unification of Germany, the nation was effectively 'Prussianised'. The renewed Germany, in the form of the Second Reich, was indisputably the creation of the Prussian army which, due to its legal status being governed by a separate constitution (*Wehrverfassung*), became effectively a State within the State. This remained in place until the constitutional changes made in 1919. From 1871 onwards, the Prussianisation of Germany was celebrated by the chief political educators, the historians, and certainly many pastors, as constituting the Will of God. This idea penetrated the minds of the majority of the population. It made Prusso-Germany into a peculiar political entity, meaning that it evinced characteristics unlike any other European state.

Consequently, Germany's political culture was heavily influenced by what the historians taught. The above-mentioned Professor Walter Peter Fuchs was convinced that if Bismarck had not nominated the fanatical Prussian nationalist and anti-Semitic Heinrich von Treitschke for the post of professor at the University of Berlin after the

---

12. Friedrich Meinecke, *Die Idee der Staatsräson in der neueren Geschichte* (Munich/ Berlin: Oldenbourg Verlag, 1929) translated as *Machiavellism:The Doctrine of Raison d'Etat and its Place in Modern Histor y* (New Haven: Yale University Press, 1957).

retirement of von Ranke in 1871,[13] and instead accepted the recommended short-listed candidate Jakob Burkhardt, a mild mannered Swiss historian of ancient Greece, the course of German history would have been dramatically different.[14] This is by no means an inconsiderable claim. It is in part answering the question why Prusso-Germany was so unlike England. The answer might be framed simply in terms that the Lutheran version of the doctrine of the divine right of kings was sustained in Germany long after it had been discarded elsewhere. If so, this was largely owing to the influence of the leading political and historical pedagogues of the Prussian school.

In Bonhoeffer's most prominent work up to 1936, namely *Nach-folge (The Cost of Discipleship)*,[15] is a passage that explicitly and unequivocally reflects the Prussian idea of the State, 'the economy of God'. Each person, from the king down to the milkmaid, slave, or prisoner, has an allocated role in God's economy. Despite their apparent bondage, they are all 'free in Christ'. Bonhoeffer here seems to be saying that through being baptised into Christ, one is equipped to comprehend freedom first on a spiritual rather than on a social plane. This means that one would be compelled by the circumstances of one's worldly existence to remain serving in whatever capacity it had pleased God to call one, whether one was a slave or a king. Here, obviously there is no eventuality or circumstance that would justify political revolution. The social-political order is presumed to be static and that is the 'economy of God'.[16]

---

13. Von Ranke had been appointed to a full professorship in Berlin in 1834, so he served in that capacity for 37 years in which time he effectively laid down the ground rules for writing the history of nation states. These have been influential ever since.

14. See Antoine Guilland, *Modern Germany and her Historians* (London: Praeger, 1970). On page 324, Guilland identifies Treitschke as a figure who 'is in the first ranks of those prophets of evil . . . a nationalist barbarian'.

15. *DBWE* 4.

16. This was certainly the bourgeois German Protestant understanding. However, in *Ethics* Bonhoeffer makes the point that a slave yearns for freedom, but he becomes a Christian before that yearning can be fulfilled. See the discussion in *Ethics*, in the 1995 Touchstone edition on 136–138. Bonhoeffer obviously agrees that all human beings yearn for freedom as something intrinsic to human nature as is the yearning for justice and peace and, of course, the basic need to be free from hunger.

This entire edifice presumes that the powers-that-be perceive themselves to be under God. Spiritual life is fulfilled simply by continuing in one's calling. It can be enriched by the study of Holy Scripture and the edifying experience of formally attending divine service, which is *Gottesdienst*. For those born in more exalted circles, one can enjoy a higher level of culture. Such a person may be edified by listening to or playing spiritual music and singing hymns. Traditionally, at Christmas and Easter in Germany, one had the opportunity of attending highly polished performances of Bach's oratorios and, as well, Mozart and Haydn masses with full orchestra and choir. These may or may not be held within a church, but wherever it is, it is *Gottesdienst,* and the listener/performer is correspondingly edified. One realises that it all presumes a very ordered background where civil society is functioning smoothly. Law and order must prevail.

Hence, beneath the perceptible similarities among Western European societies, there was, in German society, something of a subtly different order. The difference can be seen in the German concept of *Kultur* as distinct from Anglo-Saxon and Western concepts of 'civilisation' or 'culture'. The word 'culture', in English, connotes artistic and intellectual achievement and refinement, whereas, *Kultur*, in Prusso-Germany, possessed a peculiarly social and indeed racial component. It has been described by the German-Jewish professor, Georg Simmel (1858–1918), as something that not only rendered him, as a Jew, marginalised in the world of the *Bildungsbürgertum*, but moreover hindered his participation in the *Kultur* in which he lived. He came to understand that he was 'not of the blood', not a true member of the racial 'pure' community of Germans. Consequently, in order to be able to participate in *Kultur*, one had to be of undefiled German blood, in short of the *Volk*. Biology became a factor in national identity and culture. Anti-Semitism in Germany was thus not something merely attributable to Hitler and his associates; it had been deeply embedded in German *bourgeoisie* culture from much earlier times.[17]

---

17. Fritz Ringer, "'*Bildung*" The Social and Ideological Context of the German Historical Tradition', in *History of European Ideas* 10/2 (1989): 193–203.

National Socialism: The Perversion of Prusso-German Heritage

Given what has been observed about the culture of the Bismarck-ian-Wilhelmine Germany in which Bonhoeffer grew up, it becomes obvious that he found himself compelled to make a series of radical reassessments of that culture as his spiritual sensibilities developed. These reassessments constituted the pre-conditions for his later determination to join the resistance to the Third Reich. He came to see the Hitler State as a grotesque perversion of the Germany in which he had been educated, albeit one that had developed from a certain logic to be found in earlier social and political assumptions.

Bonhoeffer's intellectual-spiritual pilgrimage began at the University of Tübingen where he first enrolled in theological studies in 1923. His biographer, Eberhard Bethge, tells of his joining, briefly, an illegal paramilitary organisation known as the '*Black Reichswehr*'.[18] The organisation was a form of university regiment that had apparently appealed to him because of its patriotic sentiments. He also became a member of the very patriotic Swabian student fraternity called the *Igel* (Hedgehog) and remained affiliated to it until the fraternity drifted into endorsing extreme right-wing and anti-Semitic views. He finally resigned from it in 1936.[19]

What is illustrated here is that the young Bonhoeffer was very much identified with the values of the *Bildungsbürgertum*, extremely patriotic, and deeply resentful of the Treaty of Versailles. Although he accepted, along with his family, the new republican constitution of Weimar, as did many other *Bildungsbürger*, there was a tendency for many to remain 'monarchists at heart' (*Herzensmonarchisten*).[20] It is arguable that this characterises the young Bonhoeffer. Spiritually, he was a traditional German Lutheran and so belonged to a section of society severely disorientated by the abdication of the Kaiser and the monarchies generally. A parliamentary democratic republic was inconceivable as an *Obrigkeit*, or true authority under God. This political assumption would change as Bonhoeffer's spiritual assumptions were challenged by his theological journey.

---

18. Eberhard Bethge, *Dietrich Bonhoeffer: Theologian, Christian, Contemporary* (London: Collins, 1970).
19. Bethge, 33.
20. Friedrich Meinecke, *The German Catastrophe* (Cambridge Mass: Harvard University Press, 1950).

Bonhoeffer's Spiritual Pilgrimage

The German scholar, Adolf von Harnack (1851–1930), was the first dominant figure in Bonhoeffer's theological development. He was a family friend of the Bonhoeffers, being virtually neighbours in the leafy suburb of Grunewald, Berlin. Von Harnack was the acknowledged mentor of the so-called liberal school of theology that identified the State as the agent of Almighty God on earth. In a distinctly Hegelian way, it was argued that the struggle of nation-states for hegemony was an essential part of the divine plan for the world, the history of salvation, *Heilsgeschichte*. When the Great War broke out, the vast majority of the German academic elite, including the theologians, endorsed the War as God's Will breaking into human history in a massive apocalyptic event. Germany was apostrophised as the 'Hammer of God' and would most certainly triumph over a world of essentially barbaric and materialistic enemies.

At that time, the then young Swiss theologian, Karl Barth (1886–1968), a Social Democrat, consequently made himself very unpopular by roundly denouncing the German academic manifestos that expressed the above position. He declared it absurd that mere mortals could aspire to have deciphered the mind of the unknowable God. Thereafter, in his *Epistle to the Romans* (1918), Barth re-affirmed these accusations. From that point, von Harnack became Barth's implacable enemy. The great irony, however, was that the young Bonhoeffer had enthusiastically endorsed a small work published by Barth in 1924–1925, *Das Wort Gottes und die Theologie*. This had erected a schema of doing theology (namely, 'dialectic theology') which clearly repudiated von Harnack's 'liberal' nationalist theology. Von Harnack had, of course, strenuously maintained that his school was *scientific*, that is *wissenschaftlich*, meaning rigorously systematic and hence incontrovertible. Anything else would be disqualified as unscientific, *unwissenschaftlich*.

Nonetheless, this situation did not lead to a break between Bonhoeffer and his famous mentor, von Harnack, although the younger scholar now increasingly located himself in Barth's theological court. As a Swiss citizen of Calvinist formation, the idea that God achieved His purposes for humanity via the State was untenable to Barth. How could an institution created by fallible humans possibly be the agent of the Creator? Rather, the starting point for a new theology had to be God's *Revelation*, as laid out in Holy Scripture. These ideas infused

Bonhoeffer's 1927 doctoral and 1931 post-doctoral theses, *Sanctorum Communio* and *Akt und Sein* respectively. Remarkably, for his doctoral supervisor, Bonhoeffer had sought out the systematic theologian, Reinhold Seeberg (1859–1935), a man of fervent nationalistic convictions, although this does not seem to have influenced the way in which the thesis developed. Seeberg apparently allowed Bonhoeffer virtually complete autonomy to craft the thesis as he wished.

Politically, the atmosphere at the time, was one of acute tension owing to the radical constitutional changes and the aftermath of the great inflation that virtually pauperised the German middle classes. Indeed, the 1920s was a period of intense political recrimination in Germany, caused above all by resentment towards the Treaty of Versailles (*Versailler Diktat*) and the obligation to pay reparations. It would have taken a person of especially highly developed pacifist ideas to resist being drawn into the heated public debate. At that stage, Bonhoeffer is best understood as still a German nationalist at heart, as his talks to the German Church youth club in Barcelona graphically illustrated. In that Spanish city, where Bonhoeffer served briefly as *Vikar* (catechist) 1928–1929, the aspiring young German theologian made statements that identified him as an unreconstructed 'national liberal', justifying war as part of God's plan for humanity. Had he suddenly done a *volte face* abandoning Barth altogether by re-embracing von Harnack's position?

If we are concerned with Bonhoeffer's spiritual pilgrimage, one cannot overlook this singular episode. In talking to the young people of his congregation, that is, German expatriates, he was obviously aware that they all felt extremely resentful about the indictment of Germany entailed in the Treaty of Versailles. In this situation, Bonhoeffer seemed to sense an obligation to offer some words of consolation. In doing so, he identified most graphically with their nationalism and sense of victimhood. Had he relapsed into endorsing the war theology of *orders of creation* which was the mind-set of many Lutherans who later welcomed the advent of Hitler and the Third Reich? Consequently, one cannot speak of a linear intellectual-spiritual development from the Bonhoeffer of *Sanctorum Communio* to the Bonhoeffer who, after his sojourn at Union Seminary in New York, had become a convinced ecumenical Christian and a disciple of Karl Barth. Liberal theology (*Ordnungstheologie*) had been unceremoniously discarded.

Eberhard Bethge notes the Barcelona episode only to observe that never again did Bonhoeffer make such nationalistic statements.[21] So, here we see an individual *Bildungsbürger* in unresolved mental-spiritual turmoil. This, however, is finally resolved by the experience at Union Seminary, particularly in the encounter with the Frenchman, Jean Lasserre, the Swiss, Erwin Sutz, and the American, Paul Lehmann. Each one, in their way, was able to convince Bonhoeffer that there were no 'chosen people' anymore; God had certainly not allocated the Germans a special role in the History of Salvation. Bonhoeffer's encounter with black Americans, first with his fellow student, Frank Fisher, and then at the black Abyssinian Church in Harlem, had also a profound spiritual effect on the erstwhile *Bildungsbürger* from Berlin.

Be it noted here that people from the so-called Anglosphere sometimes have difficulty in grasping the sense of uniqueness and cultural superiority that the Teuton *Bildungsbürger* cultivated. The most famous expression of this came from Bonhoeffer's contemporary, Thomas Mann, in his 1918 book, *Bekenntnisse eines* Unpoltiischen (English: *The Reflections of a Non-Political Man)* in which he passionately extolled the virtues of Germanic culture, including over the rest of the Western sphere. The great German *Literat* soon, however, in his 1922, address, *von deutscher Republik*, distanced himself from these ultra nationalistic views even before they were trumpeted by the Nazis and considerably before his emigration to America, as did several leading intellectuals of that era.[22] Bonhoeffer, however, came to revise the values of his class through an essentially Christian theological motivation. This would have encouraged him to embrace the black American culture wholeheartedly, as his delight in their spiritual expressions illustrated. It was a learning experience that enabled him soon after to begin reassessing the traditional anti-Semitism of the German middle class.

As Bonhoeffer returned to Germany, the turmoil of the Great Depression was intensifying. The Nazis and Communists were clashing violently in the streets of all larger cities. Social Democrats and trade unionists added their weight to the protest with the aim of pre-

---

21. Bethge.
22. See Thomas Mann, 'Von Deutscher Republik', in *Gesammelte Werke* (Oldenburg: Fischer Verlag, 1960), 11: 809–852.

serving the Weimar Constitution which the extremists of both Left and Right had wished to overthrow in the realisation of their separate ideological agendas. Civil society was breaking down, especially as unemployment had reached over eight million. The outcome, despite the best efforts of the constitutionally elected governments, state and federal, was the triumph of Hitler's Party in the January 1933 national elections. The descent into the abyss had begun and, very early in 1933, Bonhoeffer began his public criticism of the new anti-constitutional, violently terrorist and racist regime. His most incisive statement was a public lecture entitled 'The Church and the Jewish Question' in April 1933 which is distinguished by its separation from Martin Luther's 1443 diatribe against the Jews, *'Von den Juden und ihren Lügen'* of which the Nazis had made much. Bonhoeffer's statement therefore merits careful investigation because it illustrates very graphically his understanding of the function of a 'legitimate' State, as opposed to the rogue State that Hitler was out to establish.

For Bonhoeffer, the Christian *Bildungsbürger*, the State under Almighty God, was there to protect the life and livelihood of all subjects, regardless of their race or religion. A State that declared war on a section of the community on those grounds was not a true State. Here, Bonhoeffer does echo Luther's doctrine of the two kingdoms, *die Zwei-Reiche-Lehre,* wherein the Church's role was to proclaim the Word of God for the spiritual welfare of the community. It was a discrete responsibility directly required by God, whereas the role of the State was to secure the kingdom and its population from chaos, be it either of internal of external origin. Above all, the State must create a situation in which all subjects are free to worship God as their tradition inspired them. If it fails in this obligation, the Church had three avenues open to it: first was to interrogate the State concerning the legitimacy of its actions; second, it could aid the victims of State action, that is, do good to all persons; third was not only to bind up the wounds of those who were crushed under the wheel of the State but also to jam a spoke into the wheel of the State; that is, to take direct political action. As Bonhoeffer put it, that 'is only possible and demanded when the Church sees the State fail in its function of creating law and order'.[23]

---

23. *Reluctant Revolutionary,* 107.

It is important to note that Bonhoeffer here is speaking as a committed Lutheran. For him, Hitler had violated the traditional Lutheran teaching on Church-State relationships; hence, arises the so-called *status confessionis*. The true faith is being undermined, so one must take a stand regardless of the consequences. This is the essential point in ascertaining Bonhoeffer's transition. His resistance to the State arises from his Lutheran formation. As Hitler intensified his persecution of the Jews in accordance with his twisted racialist convictions, Bonhoeffer saw clearly that to be consistent with the Gospel there must be vigorous opposition. The question remaining concerned the form it should take.

In one sense, Bonhoeffer was certainly a biblicist since he earnestly wrestled with the commandment, 'Thou shalt do no murder'. He grasped that Hitler was persecuting thousands of German subjects on a daily basis, and that the only way to stop it was to eliminate Hitler himself, the originator of the evil. This is not only a problem for Bonhoeffer but also for many other Lutherans, not least those in the officer corps who appreciated that what Hitler was doing would lead to the ultimate ruin of the German nation. It took some time for a core element of *Bildungsbürger* to comprehend Hitler as the enemy of the German people and therefore one who should be brought to trial for his many crimes against humanity and his reckless disregard for the likelihood that he was leading the nation to perdition.

In order for this change of mind to happen, it was necessary for the officer corps to repudiate their original oath of unconditional obedience to Hitler as *Führer*. This was not easily conceived because most would not renege on an oath once taken. Only a small number shared Bonhoeffer's conviction that Hitler was not the *Obrigkeit* which, at first, they believed him to be. Indeed, by his actions, he was an *anti-Obrigkeit* since he demanded unconditional allegiance to *his person* as leader, not under God, but to Hitler the man. As a foundation member of the Confessing Church, Bonhoeffer saw this as an untenable position for a German Lutheran.

Conclusions had to be drawn. First and foremost, Hitler had to be removed from office and arraigned before a court of law. To accomplish that, however, a sufficient number of officers would be needed to join the conspiracy to arrest Hitler and bring him to trial. When it became obvious that this pre-condition could not be achieved, the only solution was that of a *fait accompli* through the means of assassination. Bonhoeffer came to endorse this, though not without significant concerns. It seems it became a matter of crisis of conscience. In the end, he took the view that he must endorse the assassination to prevent further senseless loss of human life and then throw himself on the mercy of God.

Conclusion

Sufficient has been said to illustrate that Bonhoeffer was and remained a traditional German Lutheran and *Bildungsbürger*. His endorsement of the assassination of Hitler came out of a strictly Lutheran tradition, not by any means anything remotely Anglo-Saxon.[24] For all his appreciation of such people as the Anglican Bishop, George Bell, and the American, Reinhold Niebuhr, who both befriended him, Bonhoeffer had a problem with what he called Anglo-Saxon theology. It was suspect because of its lack of rigour and the tendency towards embracing the so-called social Gospel, like a storehouse of helpful sayings to apply in solving present day social problems. For Bonhoeffer, this was not primarily what the Gospel was about.

Of considerable significance was Bonhoeffer's progress around the Jewish question, where a pilgrimage from simply defending the Jews as fellow citizens from the injustices of the Nazi regime developed into embracing the Jews as sisters and brothers in Christ. This must be considered as a remarkable spiritual-intellectual *volte face*. Finally,

---

24. Here again the influence of the values of the *Bildungsbürgertum* is evident. Among the higher *bourgeoisie* an intrinsically German sense of *noblesse oblige* is seen operating which, of course, comes out of the Lutheran mould. See Heinz Eduard Tödt, *Komplizen, Opfer und Gegner des Hitlerregimes: Zur 'inneren Geschichte' von protestantischer Theologie und Kirche im 'Dritten Reich'*. (Gütersloh: Gütersloher Verlagshaus, 1997), 51–58. More recently see Eckart Conze, *Schatten des Kaiserreiches: Die Reichsgründung von 1871 und ihr schwieriges Erbe,* (Munich: Deutsche Taschenbuch Verein, 2020). In English the title translates as, *Shadows of the Kaiserreich; The Foundation of the Reich in 1871 and its difficult Legacy.* The author is at pains to instruct his fellow Germans today that legacy of the Prussian authoritarian constitution foisted upon the German people by Otto von Bismarck and celebrated by the highly influential Prussian school of historians led by Heinrich von Treitschke was disastrous. It was through his perception of the Bismarckian authoritarian, military state, over which Hitler had taken control so easily in retrospect, that Bonhoeffer and his few clerical associates came to rebel.

Bonhoeffer's doctrine of the State underwent a significant modification in that he came to appreciate the Anglo-Saxon idea of the rule of law to which even the *Obrigkeit* was subject. In all this, Bonhoeffer was able to learn from history, but it was a hard lesson. Above all, his openness to new impulses, whether from Italy, Spain, the United States, France, Switzerland, or England, proved crucial in his evolution into a 'theologian, Christian and contemporary'.

Breaking the Circle of the Self:
Bonhoeffer and the Religious a Priori

Peter Hooton

Introduction

John Macquarrie includes among the 'stubborn' questions raised by theology those that ask about the sources of religious knowledge, including 'the question of how far religious belief originates from a reality beyond ourselves and how far it arises out of the constitution of our own human nature.'[1] Dietrich Bonhoeffer had firm views on this issue. Knowledge of God, he believed, was grounded in the objective event of God's self-disclosure in Jesus Christ, and nowhere else. Human beings have no innate, intuitive capacity for God. There is no such thing as a purely 'religious a priori.'[2]

Bonhoeffer's critique of religious intuition faces formidable obstacles. Anyone whose faith in God springs from what is variously called positive, historical, or revealed religion will quite naturally claim that the one absolute source of religious knowledge must lie, ultimately and utterly, outside the mind. But this begs some important questions. How do we distinguish God and God's Word from vain ideas of God? How do we know when and where, in all the chaos and tumult of words, we are listening to the voice of God and not to some merely human voice? Does not the mind, as the repository and mediator of our knowing, necessarily leave that knowing open to exegesis and

---

1. John Macquarrie, *Stubborn Theological Questions* (London: SCM Press, 2003), 197.
2. The concept of the religious a priori has its origins in Kant's philosophy and was the subject of much debate among liberal Protestant theologians in the early decades of the twentieth century. Its complexities are not reflected in this article where it functions chiefly as a reasonably straightforward epistemological provocation to which Bonhoeffer responds vigorously.

thus to some ongoing degree of contestability? Bonhoeffer's position is finally sustainable only hyperbolically, but it is certainly possible to understand why he believed genuine transcendence to be incompatible with the disclosure of God through the human self-understanding. In this article, I explore Macquarrie's question in light of Bonhoeffer's critique of religious self-consciousness; and I do this, to a considerable degree, on Bonhoeffer's terms, by respecting the distinctions that lie at the heart of his theology between self and other, between boundlessness and limitation, and between the transcendental act of faith and the ontological being of revelation.

The Religious a Priori

Bonhoeffer's doctoral supervisor, Reinhold Seeberg, in his *Christian Dogmatics*, defines the religious a priori as 'a purely formal, primeval endowment of the created spirit or ego that renders it capable of, and in need of, the direct awareness of the absolute Spirit'.[3] For Seeberg, 'the supramundane' exists only 'in the religious movement of the will and intuition of the human mind'. He does not say that 'the supramundane' has no 'objective being', but insists nonetheless that it can be present to the mind 'in no other form than that of a specific, spiritual perception'.[4] All human beings are thus at least potentially open to the immediate experience of God. Seeberg assumes, as Bonhoeffer describes this in *Act and Being*, the existence of some 'mold in human beings into which the divine content of revelation, too, may pour'.[5]

Bonhoeffer strongly disagrees. If, he says, 'we are to assume that the compelling ability to receive revelation and, by implication, to believe, is given with this a priori, we have already said too much'. For Bonhoeffer, '[a]ll that pertains to personal appropriation of the fact of Christ is not a priori, but God's contingent action on human beings'. There is no specific religious quality in human beings by means of

---

3. Reinhold Seeberg, *Christliche Dogmatik* (Erlangen: Deichert, 1924–25), volume 1, 103. Cited in an editorial footnote to Bonhoeffer's letter to Eberhard Bethge of 30 April 1944. Dietrich Bonhoeffer, *Letters and Papers from Prison*, edited by John de Gruchy (Minneapolis: Fortress Press, 2010), 362, ed. fn. [11].

4. Seeberg, *Christliche Dogmatik*, Volume 1, 105. Cited in Dietrich Bonhoeffer, *Act and Being*, edited by Wayne Whitson Floyd Jr (Minneapolis: Fortress Press, 2009), 57, fn 32.

5. Bonhoeffer, *Act and Being*, 57.

which they can 'experience God's immediate contiguity in feeling and intuition'. For revelation to come to them, they must 'be changed entirely'. Natural religion has no role to play here because 'in this matter, there is no ability to hear before the hearing'. And it is God's 'concrete, preached word' that they must hear, as the only way from God to them.[6] By making a certain religious quality in humankind, rather than God's Word, the essential means of bringing human beings to the awareness of God, Seeberg renounces 'genuine transcendence . . . for a subjective immediacy, a unity in which the ability truly to distinguish between I and Other (the I and God) is lost'.[7]

I and O/other[8]

It is hard to exaggerate the significance of the I/Other distinction in Bonhoeffer's thought, where it serves both to ground human existence as such and ethical life more particularly. Human self-consciousness is embedded in the experience of duality—'the absolute duality of God and humanity'.[9] The 'I', says Bonhoeffer, 'comes into being only in relation to the You', and thus in response to an external claim.[10] Clifford Green encapsulates Bonhoeffer's thinking in 'the theological axiom that the human person always exists in relation to an Other, namely God, and that human relations are in some way analogies of this fundamental relation'.[11] There can be no self-understanding without a proper sense of exteriority, of self and other, of I and (Divine) You.

Bonhoeffer's sense of the transcendent is rooted firmly in the 'You of God' because only 'through God's active working does the other become a You to me from whom my I arises'. In other words, says Bonhoeffer, 'every human You is an image of the divine You. You-

---

6. Bonhoeffer, *Act and Being*, 58.

7. Peter Hooton, *Bonhoeffer's Religionless Christianity in Its Christological Context* (Lanham: Lexington Books/Fortress Academic, 2020), 46.

8. The upper and lower case 'o' here represent, respectively, the divine and the human.

9. Bonhoeffer, *Sanctorum Communio*, 49.

10. Dietrich Bonhoeffer, *Sanctorum Communio*, edited by Clifford Green (Minneapolis: Fortress Press, 2009), 54. From an ethical perspective, says Bonhoeffer, 'human beings do not exist 'unmediated' qua spirit in and of themselves, but only in responsibility vis-à-vis an "other"'. Bonhoeffer, *Sanctorum Communio*, 50.

11. Bonhoeffer, *Sanctorum Communio*, 50, ed. fn. 56.

character is in fact the essential form in which the divine is experienced; every human You bears its You-character only by virtue of the divine.'[12] The divine You creates the human You, 'becoming in the process, for every I, its essential experience of the transcendent—its assurance of a real outside.'[13] And this divine You confronts us 'in every step we take, in every person we meet . . . Jesus Christ, God himself, speaks to us from every human being; the other person, this enigmatic, impenetrable You, is God's claim on us.'[14] God 'becomes visible in the concrete You of social life,'[15] and Christ creates community by moving other human beings 'out of the world of things . . . and into the social sphere of persons. Only through Christ does my neighbor meet me as one who claims me in an absolute way from a position outside my existence.'[16]

As Christiane Tietz has observed, in Bonhoeffer's theology 'the other is always transcendent. He or she cannot be conceived through the I, but represents a boundary which the I encounters. . . . Only the other, who really comes from the outside, who really is *extra me*, interrupts the circle of the I and lets the I experience its boundaries.'[17] It is evident, says Michael DeJonge, that for Bonhoeffer 'what comes from outside the self must be a person rather than an idea'. Bonhoeffer's reflections on Transcendental Philosophy and Idealism have convinced him that ideas remain always 'under the power of the thinking subject. Only a person genuinely encounters the self from outside.'[18]

The Act of Faith and the Being of Revelation

The young Bonhoeffer, as Wayne Floyd describes him, was on 'a journey to discover an adequate barrier or resistance to the power

---

12. Bonhoeffer, *Sanctorum Communio*, 54–55. Italics in cited work, unless otherwise stated.
13. Hooton, *Bonhoeffer's Religionless Christianity*, 79.
14. Dietrich Bonhoeffer, 'Sermon on Matthew 28:20', in *Barcelona, Berlin, New York: 1928–1931*, edited by Clifford Green (Minneapolis: Fortress Press, 2008), 494–495.
15. Bonhoeffer, *Sanctorum Communio*, 54–55.
16. Bonhoeffer, *Act and Being*, 127.
17. Christiane Tietz, 'The Role of Jesus Christ for Christian Theology', in Michael Mawson and Philip G Ziegler, eds. *Christ, Church and World: New Studies in Bonhoeffer's Theology and Ethics* (London: Bloomsbury T&T Clark, 2016), 16.
18. Michael P DeJonge, *Bonhoeffer's Reception of Luther* (Oxford: Oxford University Press, 2017), 39.

of the intellect to try to comprehend all of reality'.[19] He wanted to leave room for the transcendent. Bonhoeffer shared Barth's conviction that there is only one way to God, which is God's way to us. He also shared Barth's sense of the enclosed and essentially circular nature of philosophical inquiry where the human being 'understands himself on the basis of his possibilities in self-reflection'.[20] Theology, on the other hand, which sees philosophy as essentially a product of the *cor curvum in se*,[21] can conceive of the human being only in relation to a boundary 'which here is called God'. Before God, 'the question about the human being becomes serious precisely because it no longer includes its own answer'. Instead, 'God gives the human being the answer completely freely and completely anew'.[22]

Philosophy may still be of occasional service to theology with which it shares 'certain general forms of thinking'.[23] Bonhoeffer points, for example, to Barth's approval of Kant's attempt to curb the boundless claims of philosophy—to limit 'reason by reason'. In Kant, he says, Barth 'finds expressed the critic of thinking upon thinking, here he sees man considered not in his full possession of transcendence but in the eternal act of referring to transcendence, man not in boundlessness, but in limitation'. Barth draws from Kant the terminology he needs 'to express the eternal crisis of man, which is brought upon him by God in Christ and which is beyond all philosophical grasp'. While philosophy and theology are both, finally, products of reflection, 'theology at least knows of an act of God, which tears man out of his reflection into an *actus directus* toward God. Here man knows himself and God not by looking into himself, but by looking to the word of God, which tells him that he is sinner and justified, which he

---

19. Wayne Whitson Floyd, 'Encounter with an Other: Immanuel Kant and GWF Hegel in the Theology of Dietrich Bonhoeffer', in *Bonhoeffer's Intellectual Formation*, edited by Peter Frick (Tübingen: Mohr Siebeck, 2008), 95–96.

20. Dietrich Bonhoeffer, 'Inaugural Lecture: The Anthropological Question in Contemporary Philosophy and Theology', in *Barcelona, Berlin, New York*, 399.

21. The heart turned in on itself.

22. Bonhoeffer, 'The Anthropological Question', 399–400.

23. Dietrich Bonhoeffer, 'The Theology of Crisis and Its Attitude toward Philosophy and Science', in *Barcelona, Berlin, New York*, 468.

never before could understand'.[24] In the *actus directus*, consciousness is focused exclusively on Christ. It has no appetite for reflection.[25] The *actus directus* is an act of faith which rests 'on the objectivity of the event of revelation in Word and sacrament'.[26] Faith is 'captivated by the gaze' of Jesus Christ; it sees only him.[27] As such, says John de Gruchy, it 'is not a certainty that we possess, but a certainty that comes to possess us, the mystery of grace that makes believing possible in the first place'.[28]

Bonhoeffer is thus convinced that we can never arrive at a reliable knowledge of reality through philosophical reflection alone. Thought, whether systematic or critical, remains self-enclosed. Only God's act of revelation can break the circle of the self and place us truly 'into reality'.[29] And revelation, as Floyd puts it, 'needs a form of thinking that both attends to the 'immediacy' of that historical particularity of revelation . . . and yet continues to distinguish itself, as thought, from the reality whose presence it mediates'.[30] This, for Bonhoeffer, is the problem of act and being, 'the issue of determining the relationship between 'the being of God' and the mental act which grasps that being', of understanding 'how faith as act, and revelation as being, are related to one another'.[31] He seeks an epistemology that 'transcends the desire of the knower to grasp and control the object of knowledge'[32] and draws for this purpose on Kant's distinction between our systematic ordering of the different elements of experience and the 'thing-in-itself' which lies outside this experience. This allows Bon-

---

24. Bonhoeffer, 'Theology of Crisis', 473–74. The Christian message, says Bonhoeffer, comes 'entirely from outside of the world of sin'. God comes in Jesus Christ and 'breaks as the holy Ghost into the circle of man, not as a new idea, a new value by virtue of which man could save himself, but in concreteness as judgment and forgiveness of sin . . . The whole existence of man in his egocentric world has to be shaken before man can see God as really outside of himself.' Bonhoeffer, 'Theology of Crisis', 473.

25. Dietrich Bonhoeffer, *Act and Being*, edited by Wayne Floyd (Minneapolis: Fortress Press, 2009), 100.

26. Bonhoeffer, *Act and Being*, 158.

27. Dietrich Bonhoeffer, *Ethics*, ed. Clifford J Green (Minneapolis: Fortress Press, 2005), 147.

28. John W. de Gruchy, *Led into Mystery* (London: SCM Press, 2013), 120.

29. Bonhoeffer, *Act and Being*, 90.

30. Wayne Floyd, Editor's Introduction, *Act and Being*, 17.

31. Bonhoeffer, *Act and Being*, 27–28.

32. Floyd, Editor's Introduction, *Act and Being*, 8.

hoeffer to maintain a relationship between the act of thinking (which affords authentic but only partial knowledge of reality) and something 'ontologically distinct from the thinking subject',[33] and thus, theologically speaking, a balance between the transcendental act of faith and the ontological being of revelation. God's revelation, says Floyd, 'names that situation of openness where reality is always and only to be understood "in reference to" the thinking subject, whose process of thought is ontologically 'suspended' in being that it has not created'.[34]

The Critique of Religious Inwardness

Bonhoeffer's critique of Seeberg's religious a priori takes its cue from Barth's Word of God theology. It echoes Barth's repudiation of liberal theology's associations with Schleiermacher's subjective religious epistemology, where the religious a priori may perhaps be said to provide the formal condition of sensibility for Schleiermacher's intuitive experience of the divine.[35]

As a young man, Barth could speak more highly of no other theologian than Schleiermacher. When, however, Barth found himself driven to abandon liberal Protestant theology[36] and to re-imagine the nature and task of theology for himself, he came to see in the architect of nineteenth century liberal Protestantism the perfect foil for a new approach to dogmatics, the focus of which would be God's concrete self-disclosure in the Word. Barth wanted nothing less than a 'theological revolution'[37] to reclaim theology from its preoccupation with

---

33. Floyd, Editor's Introduction, *Act and Being*, p. 10.
34. Floyd, "Encounter with an Other," p. 103.
35. Mark D. Chapman (2001), *Ernst Troeltsch and Liberal Theology: Religion and Cultural Synthesis in Wilhelmine Germany* (Oxford Scholarship Online, October 2011), p. 112. DOI: 10.1093/acprof:oso/9780199246427.001.0001. Accessed 30 August 2021.
36. One strong reason for this, following the outbreak of war in 1914, was the publication of a manifesto, signed, inter alia, by almost all of Barth's German teachers, supporting "the war policy of Kaiser Wilhelm II." While Barth did not believe that Schleiermacher would have signed such a manifesto, "it was still the case that the entire theology which had unmasked itself in that manifesto . . . was grounded, determined, and influenced decisively by him." Karl Barth, *The Theology of Schleiermacher* (Edinburgh: T & T Clark, 1982), p. 264.
37. Barth, *Theology of Schleiermacher*, p. 259.

'the human subject of faith to its divine object and proper ground'.[38] He sought to recover a proper sense of God's transcendence and to ground human experience of the divine in an actual event: the act of revelation. In Barth's theology, 'God's being, or truth, is the event of his self-disclosure'.[39] God drives the relationship between God and human beings. Turn this around and theology becomes 'the prisoner of some sort of anthropology or ontology that is an underlying interpretation of existence, of faith, or of man's spiritual capacity'.[40] And this, of course, is precisely what Barth believes Schleiermacher to have done. For Schleiermacher, the essence of religion is to be found neither in metaphysics (thinking) nor morals (acting) but rather, in the youthful speeches *On Religion*, in intuition and feeling[41] and later, in *The Christian Faith*, in the sense of absolute dependence[42] which, as Barth describes it, draws 'intuition' into 'feeling', thereby abolishing the earlier distinction[43]—and 'in whose place of course one could then set "faith" in order to move somewhat closer to the Bible or the Reformation'.[44]

Schleiermacher's intuition is always 'something individual, set apart, the immediate perception, nothing more'.[45] In religion it is the universe that is intuited—that is 'posited as originally acting on us'—and whether God is present to the religious intuition 'depends on the direction of the imagination'.[46] Intuition is the expression of religion's 'sensibility and taste for the infinite'.[47] It facilitates a recognition of the influence upon us of the independent actions of the universe by allowing the one who intuits 'to accept everything individual as a part of the whole and everything limited as a representation of

---

38. Alan Spence, *Christology: A Guide for the Perplexed* (London: T & T Clark, 2008), p. 129.
39. Karl Barth, *Evangelical Theology: An Introduction* (Grand Rapids, MI: Eerdmans, 1979), 9.
40. Barth, *Evangelical Theology*, 8.
41. Friedrich Schleiermacher, *On Religion: Speeches to its Cultured Despisers* (Cambridge: Cambridge University Press, 1996), 22.
42. Friedrich Schleiermacher, *The Christian Faith*, edited by HR Mackintosh and JS Stewart (Edinburgh: T&T Clark, 1928), 1/4, 12.
43. Barth, *Theology of Schleiermacher*, 271.
44. Barth, *Theology of Schleiermacher*, 269.
45. Schleiermacher, *On Religion*, 26.
46. Schleiermacher, *On Religion*, 51–53.
47. Schleiermacher, *On Religion*, 23.

the infinite.'[48] Intuition and feeling are connected because 'the same actions of the universe through which it reveals itself to you in the finite also bring it [via the senses] into a new relationship to your mind and your condition.'[49] There is, for Barth, in Schleiermacher's enterprise more philosophy than theology; more Plato and Spinoza than Aristotle and Kant; an almost incidental Christianity; and the sense that people 'feel, think, and speak in and from a sovereign consciousness that their own beings are . . . essentially united with everything which might possibly come into question as something or even someone distinct from them.'[50]

Barth, on the other hand, is concerned exclusively with theology and with an 'object toward which adoration, gratitude, repentance, and supplication are concretely possible and even imperative.'[51] He seeks to comprehend 'a specific *object* and its environment . . . on its own terms and to speak of it along with all the implications of its *existence*'. As such, the word 'theology' signifies 'a very special science, whose task is to apprehend, understand, and speak of God.'[52] It presupposes only 'God's own proof of his existence and sovereignty' and is in every other respect a free science, depending on no anterior anthropological or ontological assumptions. The relationship is one of 'man to *God*' rather than of 'God to *man*'.[53] Only God can reveal God and nothing in nature or in philosophy prepares us for this.

Whereas Schleiermacher grounds the knowledge of God in the human self-understanding, Barth's theology is rooted firmly in the apprehension of God's revelation in its historicity. The object of theology is 'God in the *history* of his *deeds*'.[54] God's self-disclosure in the act of revelation is 'the most concrete reality for man'[55] and has a unique identity of its own. As Hans Urs von Balthasar observes, 'we can never reach the particular and the distinctive by starting out from the general. For we must *start with the particular and try to evaluate*

---

48. Schleiermacher, *On Religion*, 24–25.
49. Schleiermacher, *On Religion*, 29.
50. Barth, *Theology of Schleiermacher*, 275.
51. Barth, *Theology of Schleiermacher*, 275.
52. Barth, *Evangelical Theology*, 3.
53. Barth, *Evangelical Theology*, 8.
54. Barth, *Evangelical Theology*, 9.
55. Hans Urs von Balthasar, *The Theology of Karl Barth* (New York: Holt, Rinehart and Winston, 1971), 165.

everything else from there.[56] Theology speaks of the consummation of God's Word in 'the Christ of Israel' where it 'has become *particular*, that is, Jewish flesh' whose saving grace 'applies *universally* to all men'.[57] And this Word is nowhere more plainly visible than in the divine act of resurrection—the world's kairotic moment—to which theology is required faithfully to witness and attest.

Barth thus strove to see Jesus as 'he was seen by the community in which the New Testament arose'.[58] This was, of course, a post-resurrection community and Barth consequently made 'no attempt to see and understand [Jesus'] life prior to his death as if it were not illuminated and interpreted . . . by what happened after his death, as if we were later free to see and represent it either in this light, in one like it, or in a very different light'.[59] Barth's whole theology rests on the truth of the resurrection and on the presence of 'a living Lord who summons, instructs, commands and saves'.[60] This, for Barth, is the one real world of the Bible, which is also our world. As David Ford observes, in Barth's theology the early years of the first millennium are 'eternalized'. They encompass 'all history'.[61] The life of Jesus Christ provides us with an overarching story which is also our story. Post-Enlightenment theories of the self, 'especially those which pivot on the human subject of experience', are replaced by the 'true self . . . now described in a series of events told in a realistic story'.[62]

In Schleiermacher's vision of reality, on the other hand, positive (historical; revealed) religion and natural religion may be understood to occupy the extreme ends of a great series.[63] The historical religions 'proceed from a living intuition of the universe' and this is

---

56. von Balthasar, *Theology of Karl Barth*, 166.
57. Barth, *Evangelical Theology*, 23.
58. Barth, *Church Dogmatics IV/2*, edited by GW Bromiley and TF Torrance (London: T&T Clark, 1999), 247.
59. Barth, *Church Dogmatics IV/2*, 248.
60. Katherine Sonderegger, 'Et Resurrexit Tertia Die: Jenson and Barth on Christ's Resurrection', in *Conversing with Barth*, eds. John McDowell and Mike Higton, (Aldershot: Ashgate Publishing, 2004), 191.
61. David Ford, *Barth and God's Story* (Frankfurt am Main: Verlag Peter Main, 1981), 25.
62. Ford, *Barth and God's Story*, 168.
63. David Klemm, 'Culture, Arts and Religion', in *The Cambridge Companion to Friedrich Schleiermacher*, edited by Jacqueline Mariña (Cambridge: Cambridge University Press, 2005), 255; Schleiermacher, *On Religion*, 6.

their strength.[64] Natural religion, meanwhile, is better able to grasp what the historical religions have in common. Its strength lies in its breadth of understanding. But, as David Klemm observes, Schleiermacher is also cognisant of the limitations of both and believes neither historical religion nor natural religion to be in fact what it believes itself to be. Historical religion claims to have revealed knowledge but is really 'capable only of offering opinions and beliefs', while natural religion claims to 'ground religion in metaphysics or morals' but is really just 'abstract and formal reasoning' with 'no basic intuition and feeling of the universe of its own'. Schleiermacher, says Klemm, wants us to 'rise above' these forms of religion to a philosophical theology which 'rightly comprehends both the historical religions and natural religion from the inside, as human phenomena that constitute real forces within culture, while criticizing one-sided attachments to particularity (in positive religion) or universality (in natural religion)'.[65]

While Schleiermacher thus holds the particular and the universal together in creative tension, Barth takes an extreme stand at one end of the spectrum of possibilities. For Barth, there is only historical, revealed religion. Indeed, there is only *one* revealed religion and intuition has no place in it. Schleiermacher seeks a synthesis in which Barth is simply not interested. In fact, he is irritated by Schleiermacher's determination to establish harmony—a harmony of Christianity and culture—where there can be none. Schleiermacher, Barth contends, 'strives against all strife'[66] 'The uniting of what is divided, the reconciling of what is opposed, communion between those that differ—this seems to be . . . the concern which ultimately motivates him.'[67] Schleiermacher, on the other hand, understands his reconciliatory theory of religion to coincide, as Stephen Sykes says, 'with the actual substance of Christianity's fundamental idea, the divine reconciliation of the innate hostility and resistance of all finite things to the unity of the whole.'[68]

---

64. Klemm, 'Culture, arts and religion', 261.
65. Klemm, 'Culture, arts and religion', 257–62.
66. Barth, *Theology of Schleiermacher*, 39.
67. Barth, *Theology of Schleiermacher*, 11.
68. Stephen Sykes, 'Schleiermacher and Barth on the Essence of Christianity—an Instructive Disagreement', in *Barth and Schleiermacher: Beyond the Impasse?* edited by James Duke and Robert Streetman (Philadelphia: Fortress Press, 1988), 93.

The Place of Interiority

In the speeches *On Religion*, Schleiermacher's God-consciousness is given in what Jacqueline Mariña calls 'a moment of immediate awareness that precedes the subject's awareness of itself *as* a subject over against a world of objects'. In this moment, there is neither subject nor object, neither self nor idea. God is present as intuition and 'apprehended through feeling; no concept can ever be adequate to it'.[69] Later, in *The Christian Faith*, where Schleiermacher describes God-consciousness as the feeling of absolute dependence, 'any possibility of God being in any way given is entirely excluded because anything that is outwardly given must be given as an object exposed to our counter-influence, however slight this may be'.[70] The feeling of absolute dependence can have nothing in the world as its object. It is rather the '*Whence* of our receptive and active existence'—the ground of our being—which is neither the world in its totality nor any single part of it.[71] There is thus an important sense in which, as Mariña says, 'the feeling of absolute dependence is logically *prior* to experience of the world, since it does not arise from it'.[72] All knowledge of God—including general and particular revelation, and everything that flows from them—is rooted in an experience which has no conceptual, and certainly no doctrinal, foundation.

It is I think reasonable to categorise Schleiermacher's religious 'feeling' as mystical in orientation. As Christine Helmer points out, Schleiermacher, in a letter written three years after the publication of the first edition of *On Religion*, spoke of '"the mystical predisposition that was an essential part" of his individuality'.[73] She is wary though of the preconceptual—and thus necessarily pre-Christian—space from which Mariña's careful description of Schleiermacher's intuition and feeling emerges. Indeed she insists that, even in the early writings where there is certainly evidence of a disposition to dissolve

---

69. Jacqueline Mariña, 'Friedrich Schleiermacher and Rudolf Otto', in *The Oxford Handbook of Religion and Emotion*, edited by John Corrigan (Oxford University Press, Online Publication Date: Sep 2009), 459. DOI: 10.1093/oxfordhb/9780195170214.003.0026. Accessed 8 September 2020.

70. Schleiermacher, *Christian Faith*, 1.4, 18.

71. Schleiermacher, *Christian Faith*, 1.4, 16.

72. Mariña, 'Schleiermacher and Otto', 459.

73. Christine Helmer, 'Mysticism and Metaphysics: Schleiermacher and a Historical-Theological Trajectory', in *The Journal of Religion*, 83/4 (October 2003): 528.

the finite into the infinite, the 'interpersonal context' is already 'the privileged site for the mystical intuition of the universe'. Mysticism, says Helmer, is here 'neither solipsistic interiority nor the immediacy of the infinite, but the universe mediated by external means through which the universe has chosen to disclose itself'.[74] The later key to understanding this lies in the ecclesiastically-mediated relationship of the individual believer to Jesus Christ where, for Schleiermacher, 'Christ's redemptive activity effects simultaneously the new creation of the individual and the constitution of the community'.[75] As such, the 'mystical element', at least in Schleiermacher's later work, is consistently determined 'in explicitly Christian theological terms'.[76]

Gorazd Andrejč argues that although, for Schleiermacher, religious feelings can be of more than one kind, one and only one 'very special' kind—which is the kind that entails 'some degree of "losing" oneself in a deep relation with the whole'—characterises the essence of religion.[77] As Schleiermacher says: 'Recall how in religion everything strives to expand the sharply delineated outlines of our personality and gradually to lose them in the infinite in order that we, by intuiting the universe, will become one with it as much as possible'.[78] But our nonindividuated intuitions of the universe are with us only momentarily and their value lies less in their largely 'indescribable' content[79] than in the sense of possibility they engender. In the brief but profound 'communion between a person and the universe'[80] lies the seed of 'phenomenologically more complex' feelings of the social mystical kind described by Helmer. These more specifically Christian feelings are associated with 'a "person-forming" process that happens in the Christ-believing community'.[81] Religion is thus never purely intuitive and God-consciousness is never entirely content-free. Reli-

74. Helmer, 'Mysticism and Metaphysics', 531.
75. Helmer, 'Mysticism and Metaphysics', 533.
76. Helmer, 'Mysticism and Metaphysics', 536.
77. Gorazd Andrejč, 'Bridging the Gap Between Social and Existential-Mystical Interpretations of Schleiermacher's "feeling,"', in *Religious Studies* (2012) 48 (Cambridge University Press 2012), 389.
78. Schleiermacher, *On Religion*, 53.
79. Schleiermacher, *On Religion*, 31.
80. Schleiermacher, *On Religion*, 59.
81. Andrejč, 'Bridging the gap', 392.

gious experience is for Schleiermacher always finally 'a *situated experience* of the transcendent'.[82]

Bonhoeffer's dismissal of the religious a priori in Seeberg's *Christliche Dogmatik* naturally separates him from Schleiermacher's claim that religion 'springs necessarily and by itself from the interior of every soul'.[83] With this claim, revelation loses its external character. Genuine transcendence is replaced by a self-enclosed, subjective immediacy and the principal topic of theology becomes the human self-consciousness—the religious state of mind. Schleiermacher, says Bonhoeffer, 'established the proper territory of religion by localizing religion in the religious province of the soul'.[84] Religion became something partial. It no longer addressed the whole human being.

The conviction that human beings are innately religious is facilitated by a mystical disposition that Bonhoeffer does not share. He is suspicious of the religious endeavour to achieve any form of unity with God 'on one's own initiative and based on one's own divine potential'. Such initiatives, he believes, not only fail to take account of 'the humanly unbridgeable gulf between God and human beings'[85] but also violate the all-important 'boundary of the I-You-relation', which is basic to Bonhoeffer's theology and to his understanding of the nature of human existence.[86] Union with God is incompatible with a concept of personhood grounded in the human being's relation to God as archetypal Other. As such, there can be no 'final assimilation into God's all-encompassing person'.[87] Human beings 'are never lost in God, or in one another'.[88] An ethical sociality, far from precluding singularity, actually requires it. Mysticism shares with Idealism the

---

82. Jacqueline Mariña, 'Schleiermacher on the Outpourings of the Inner Fire', in *Religious Studies,* 40 (2004): 133; cited in Andrejč, 'Bridging the gap', in *Religious Studies,* 393.

83. Schleiermacher, *On Religion,* p. 17.

84. Dietrich Bonhoeffer, "The History of Twentieth-Century Systematic Theology (Student Notes)," in *Ecumenical, Academic, and Pastoral Work: 1931–1932,* edited by Victoria J Barnett, Mark S Brocker, and Michael B Lukens (Minneapolis: Fortress Press, 2012), 184–185.

85. Dietrich Bonhoeffer, 'Jesus Christ and the Essence of Christianity', in *Barcelona, Berlin, New York,* 356.

86. Bonhoeffer, *Sanctorum Communio,* 84.

87. Bonhoeffer, *Sanctorum Communio,* 287.

88. Hooton, *Bonhoeffer's Religionless Christianity,* 144.

propensity to relate the I to itself 'in unmediated reflection' and, in this way, it locks God, too, into human consciousness.[89]

Bonhoeffer is never though, in fact, far from the Christ-centred sense of interiority which, though very differently expressed, is also characteristic of Schleiermacher's theology. In a youthful sermon, Bonhoeffer speaks of the need to give the soul respite from the chaos of life by surrendering to 'the superior power of the other, the wholly other'. The soul is silent before God, ready to hear, and to obey, God's will.[90] And he begins the Christology lectures by invoking the "silence of the church" before the Word. 'In proclaiming Christ, the church falls on its knees in silence before the inexpressible.'[91] There is a wealth of feeling, too, in the biblical reflection on the break of day, written for the ordinands at Finkenwalde in the summer of 1935, where 'each new morning' represents 'a new beginning for our lives'. As such,

> [i]t is not our own plans and worries . . . that should fill the first moments of each new day, but rather God's liberating grace, God's blessed nearness . . . Before the heart opens itself up to the world, God wishes to open it up to God's gaze; before the ear perceives the innumerable voices of the day, it should hear the voice of the Creator and Redeemer in the early morning.[92]

In Bonhoeffer's writings the mystical element is subsumed in a numinous openness to the revealed Word of God. There may well be for him no innate, intuitive human capacity for God, but there is nonetheless a depth in people where the holy encounter with God takes place.

Conclusion

Bonhoeffer firmly believes our knowledge of God to be grounded solely in the objective event of God's self-disclosure in Jesus Christ. Truth is not to be found in the human self-understanding. We must

89. Bonhoeffer, *Act and Being*, 53.
90. Dietrich Bonhoeffer, 'Sermon on Psalm 62:2', in *Barcelona, Berlin, New York*, pp. 501-2.
91. Dietrich Bonhoeffer, 'Lectures on Christology', in *Berlin: 1932-1933*, edited by Larry Rasmussen (Minneapolis: Fortress Press, 2009), 300.
92. Dietrich Bonhoeffer, 'Biblical Reflection: Morning', in *Theological Education at Finkenwalde: 1935-1937*, edited by Gaylon Barker and Mark Brocker (Minneapolis: Fortress Press, 2013), 864-865.

rather, as Thomas Torrance observes, "look for it beyond ourselves in God";[93] in God's self-revelation which "is to be apprehended . . . in the light of its actual happening in our midst and through a conceptual assent which we are forced to yield to it under its own evidence."[94] Human beings have no inherent capacity for God. There is no purely religious a priori. Only through God's revelation—as God's way to us—is there any real contact between God and human beings.

In Bonhoeffer's theology, this thoroughly Barthian conviction is rooted in "the absolute duality of God and humanity"[95] and supported by an ethic of existence which hinges on the I's response to an external claim—the claim of Jesus Christ who confronts us "in every step we take, in every person we meet."[96] The encounter with Jesus Christ—"the human being for others"—is the experience of transcendence. It is "a genuine experience of God."[97] Bonhoeffer's theology, like Schleiermacher's, is grounded in experience, but it is an experience of otherness, of distinction, rather than of union. Here the self experiences its limits. There is no prospect of its gradual dissolution in the infinite.[98] God's revelation facilitates a relationship between the act of thinking and something "ontologically distinct from the thinking subject"[99]—a balance between the transcendental act of faith and the ontological being of revelation.

Seeberg, on the other hand, clearly understands that we can no more get behind the mind than we can get behind God. He seeks to overcome God's unknowability—God's transcendent Otherness—by positing a "primeval endowment of the created spirit . . . that renders it capable of . . . the direct awareness of the absolute Spirit."[100] The religious a priori opens a way to God that we would not otherwise have. Bonhoeffer sees in this "a turning away" from pure transcendentalism towards an idealism in which all real sense of transcendence is

---

93. Thomas Torrance, *God and Rationality* (Edinburgh: T&T Clark, 1997), p. 68.
94. Torrance, *God and Rationality*, p. 67.
95. Bonhoeffer, *Sanctorum Communio*, p. 49.
96. Bonhoeffer, "Sermon on Matthew 28:20," p. 494.
97. Bonhoeffer, *Letters and Papers*, p. 501.
98. Schleiermacher, *On Religion*, p. 53.
99. Floyd, Editor's Introduction, *Act and Being*, p. 10.
100. Seeberg, *Christliche Dogmatik*, Vol. 1, p. 103. Cited in Bonhoeffer, *Letters and Papers*, p. 362, ed. fn. [11].

lost in the I.[101] He believes Seeberg's argument to be both wrong and unnecessary. All knowledge of God is the result of "God's contingent action on human beings" and, to understand this, we need "no other forms of thought than are supplied by the pure a priori of thought itself."[102] The search for God, Bonhoeffer insists, can begin only after God has revealed God's self to the seeker. There is no blind quest for God. Those who truly search for God "already know who God is."[103] There is no room in Bonhoeffer's theology either for Seeberg's religious a priori or for Schleiermacher's exclusion of the "possibility of God being in any way [outwardly] given."[104]

When all is said and done, these competing claims have something very important in common: a shared affirmation of God's final ineffability. And they help us understand why Macquarrie does not pose an "either/or" question; why he asks only "*how far* religious belief originates from a reality beyond ourselves and *how far* it arises out of the constitution of our own human nature"?[105] There can be, of course, humanly speaking, no one right answer to this question. Macquarrie might even perhaps be accused of promoting a false dichotomy. There is, after all—from both a theological and a philosophical point of view—no good reason to doubt either the existence of a real outside or the fact that we have no finally reliable (which is to say incontrovertibly "objective") access to it. I have no desire, though, to obscure what I believe to be a valuable distinction between the irrefragable Word of God and the contested manner of its reception. The distinction is redolent of the experience of duality which, in Bonhoeffer's radically relational theology, underpins the human being's understanding of existence as such.

I conclude this article with two observations of an essentially, and I think fittingly, ethical—rather than epistemological or dogmatic—character. First, Bonhoeffer's insistence on the reality of the everyday encounter with Jesus Christ speaks to the need for people to bring their religious beliefs into meaningful and compassionate relationship with the whole of life in the world. Western Christianity seems more or less oblivious to the gap that has opened up between

---

101. Bonhoeffer, *Act and Being*, p. 58.
102. Bonhoeffer, *Act and Being*, p. 58.
103. Bonhoeffer, "Lectures on Christology," p. 303.
104. Schleiermacher, *Christian Faith*, 1.4, p. 18.
105. Macquarrie, *Stubborn Theological Questions*, p. 197. My italics.

the highly individualised sense of God's salvific presence and the all-inclusive, agapeic substance of the Word.[106] In this situation, it helps to be reminded that—however imperfectly we may understand this—God's undivided Word comes, originally and constantly, from a "place" outside ourselves, and that it is not as such at our disposal.

It has always been much too easy, though, to lose all sense of God's inclusivity in the struggle to promote particular ideas of God. In this situation, the "assenting certainty" that roots faith in God in religious feeling rather than in the assumed "truth of any conceptualized doctrinal formulation"[107] gives to religion, at least potentially, a space and tolerance that the historical witness and its derivative beliefs and traditions do not easily accommodate. Schleiermacher's critique of "one-sided attachments to particularity (in positive religion) [and] universality (in natural religion)"[108] has, I would suggest, an enduring place in Christian theology.

---

106. The privatisation of faith facilitates the compartmentalisation of religion. Barry Harvey draws attention to what he describes as an essentially secular process of cultural engineering—the division of culture into "autonomous value spheres (science, religion, morality, art)"—by means of which religion, "as a private facet of human experience," becomes a mechanism for confining faith to a particular space "within the contours and dynamics of modernity." Barry A. Harvey, "A Post-Critical Approach to 'Religionless Christianity,'" in Wayne Whitson Floyd Jr. and Charles Marsh, eds. *Theology and the Practice of Responsibility: Essays on Dietrich Bonhoeffer* (Valley Forge, PA: Trinity Press International, 1994), pp. 39, 47.

107. Robert Merrihew Adams, "Faith and Religious Knowledge," in Jacqueline Mariña, ed. *The Cambridge Companion to Friedrich Schleiermacher* (Cambridge: Cambridge University Press, 2005), p. 42.

108. Klemm, "Culture, arts and religion," p. 262.

Vol 8 No 1/2020

Reading the Luther Bible with Dietrich Bonhoeffer

Joel Looper

Introduction

Scripture shaped Dietrich Bonhoeffer's understanding of reality and the language he used in his writings. This essay argues that unless the Luther Bible, which was Bonhoeffer's Bible, is read alongside the Bonhoeffer corpus, readers may miss significant allusions and details in his work. It also offers two insights gained from this practice. The first seems to provide confirmation that Bonhoeffer implied that Adolf Hitler was the Antichrist in a radio address known as 'The Führer and the Individual in the Younger Generation.' The second discusses an allusion to Philippians 3 in Bonhoeffer's poem 'Stations on the Way to Freedom.'

How Bonhoeffer Read Scripture

'It should not be forgotten,' Eberhard Bethge wrote of his friend, how Bonhoeffer used his Bible for prayer. He thought that one should sit and listen prayerfully to the Bible, to hear whatever voice would speak. This meant that the I, the Today, the contemporary world and their voices had to remain silent, so that the person praying would become immersed in the world of the biblical verse and thus become involved in biblical salvation history. This is similar to how Jews read the story of the liberation from Egypt and the time in which they read it. And so when he was praying with the Scriptures, Bonhoeffer never actually referred to his world, with its dates and catchwords, in his marginal jottings, although he always

had a pencil in his hand to mark things in the printed word
that became important . . .[1]

Perhaps this is why, apart from a reference to *Kristallnacht* ('9.11.38')
next to Psalm 74:8, 'there is not a single note in his Bible giving a date
or key word for something contemporary or of political or family or
personal importance.'[2]

This does not mean that Bonhoeffer's world was bifurcated
between real life and religious life or, perhaps, between life where
one acts responsibly according to the situation at hand and life where
one believes idealistically according to one's religious commitments.
Far from it. Neither did Bonhoeffer consciously foist his own life and
problems onto the text of Scripture. Instead, Bonhoeffer's view of the
world around him was itself decisively shaped by his reading of the
Bible. In *Life Together* he could write,

> It is not that God's help and presence must still be proved in our
> life; rather God's presence and help have been demonstrated
> for us in the life of Jesus Christ. It is in fact more important for
> us to know what God did to Israel, in God's son Jesus Christ,
> than to discover what God intends for us today. The fact that
> Jesus Christ died is more important than the fact that I will die
> . . . I find salvation not in my life story, but only in the story of
> Jesus Christ. Only those who allow themselves to be found in
> Jesus Christ—in the incarnation, cross, and resurrection—are
> with God and God with them . . . What we call our life, our
> troubles, and our guilt are by no means the whole of reality;
> our life, our need, our guilt, and our deliverance are there in

---

1. Eberhard Bethge, 'One of the Silent Bystanders?', in *Friendship and Resistance:
    Essays on Dietrich Bonhoeffer* (Grand Rapids: Eerdmans, 1995), 64.
2. *Kristallnacht*, often referred to in English as 'the night of broken glass,' had
    happened the night of 9–10 November. Perhaps Bonhoeffer's marginal note
    does not reflect that date because he did not hear about the terrors of that
    night until 11 November. Synagogues were burned, Jewish homes attacked,
    and Jewish businesses ransacked across Germany in an event that shocked the
    world. Though dozens of Jews were murdered in the pogrom and about 30,000
    Jewish men arrested and taken to Dachau, Buchenwald, and Sachsenhausen,
    the Confessing Church remained silent. See Richard Evans, *The Third Reich in
    Power* (New York: Penguin, 2005), 580–597 and Victoria Barnett, *For the Soul of
    the People: Protestant Protest Against Hitler* (New York: Oxford University Press,
    1992), 155–156.

the Scriptures. Because it pleased God to act for us there, it is only there that we will be helped. Only in the Holy Scriptures do we get to know our own story. The God of Abraham, Isaac, and Jacob is the God and Father of Jesus Christ and our God.[3]

Such a view of life could only be held by someone simply steeped in both the stories and the language of the Scriptures, and this, in turn, has consequences for how Bonhoeffer's theology should be approached. Without a determination to read his writings with Scripture constantly in view, one cannot hope to successfully grapple with either his theological intent in innumerable critical passages or the theological, ecclesial, and political implications Bonhoeffer himself believed his work to have.

The Luther Bible

First and foremost, if the Scriptures shaped Bonhoeffer in this way, then those who read him would do well to keep the Luther Bible at their elbow. That, after all, was Bonhoeffer's Bible. It had formed Bonhoeffer through a lifetime of study and through meditation on the Moravian daily texts (*Die Losungen*); it had also formed the German language and culture that Bonhoeffer called home and the German church he served.[4] One simply cannot adequately approach the subject of this paper—the Scriptural cast of Bonhoeffer's theology—without familiarizing oneself with the Luther Bible.

The Luther Bible was conceived in December 1521 when friends of Luther visited him in a castle in Saxony where, having been condemned by the church and outlawed by the Empire at the Diet of Worms the previous May, he was kept in protective custody by Elector Frederick the Wise. Luther flew through the initial stage of the project, translating the entire New Testament in eleven weeks, and *The New Testament in German (Das neue Tyestament Deutsch)*

---

3. Bonhoeffer, *DBWE 5*, 62. Though I would argue that Bonhoeffer continues to hold a similar stance toward the Scriptural narrative and the world even in the prison letters, one can read those letters differently and still find the observations below helpful.

4. Today other translations such as *Einheitsübersetzung* are also used in the Moravian readings. Modern translations like this one, which was authorized by Vatican II, were not yet on the horizon during Bonhoeffer's lifetime.

appeared in late September 1522.[5] Though Luther had not been named as the translator, the matter quickly became known, and the Bible sold so well that the Wittenberg printer Melchior Lotther the Younger became quite rich.

The rest of the project took Luther somewhat longer. The Pentateuch appeared in 1523 and the Historical books the next year. But the minor prophets, the book of Isaiah and the other major prophets, the wisdom literature (particularly Job), and the Deuterocanonical literature took much longer, and, though Melanchthon and others assisted him, prefaces and marginal notes also had to be written. The immensity of the project and the many other demands on his time caught up with Luther; publication would have to wait until 1534. When it did finally come to market, however, the Bible was a stunning success nonetheless. According to Eric Gritsch, by the time Luther died in 1546 half a million of these Bibles had been sold.[6]

There had been previous German translations of the Bible, but Luther's translation quickly eclipsed these for several reasons. First, Johannes Gutenberg's introduction of movable type to Europe and his invention of the printing press had only happened a half century before in 1466. The mass production of books was then a relatively recent phenomenon, so competition was limited. Secondly, political intrigue by electors against Holy Roman Emperor Charles V, a devoted Catholic, made space for the dissemination of the new translation. Finally, Luther's renown and, later, the theological authority associated with his name played an enormous role in his Bible's popularity. Thus the Luther Bible became the most influential book in the German-speaking world, shaping German culture analogously to the way the King James translation would shape the Anglophone world.

One is therefore likely to find allusions to the Luther Bible everywhere in the Bonhoeffer corpus, including in those places where one might not expect him to have Scripture in mind and even in passages that initially appear purely 'political.' Presumably allusions made their way into his writings that Bonhoeffer himself did not consciously intend. Thumb through any volume of the *Dietrich Bonhoeffer Works*

---

5. Eric W Gritsch, 'Luther as Bible Translator', in *The Cambridge Companion to Martin Luther*, edited by Donald K McKim (Cambridge: Cambridge University Press, 2003), 63–64.

6. Luther himself apparently never asked for and never received any royalties. Gritsch, 'Luther as Bible Translator,' 71.

in German, pick a Scriptural quotation or reference at random, and it is very likely to be from the Luther Bible.[7] Sometimes the reader will realize that the Luther Bible on her shelf does not correspond to the 1545 edition that Bonhoeffer had in mind; occasionally she will find that Bonhoeffer is using another translation altogether or merely alluding to the text in question without quoting it precisely.[8] For these reasons, those who want to trace Bonhoeffer's dependence upon Scripture should proceed with care. Nevertheless, readers of Bonhoeffer stand to gain new insights from increased attention to the specific language of Luther's translation, and sometimes, at least for those who care about Bonhoeffer's legacy, those insights can be significant.

Hitler as Antichrist

Take, for example, the radio address Bonhoeffer gave at 5:45 p.m. on 1 February, 1933 that appears in the *Dietrich Bonhoeffer Works* English translation under the title 'The Führer and the Individual in the Younger Generation.'[9] To Bonhoeffer's annoyance, the radio transmission was suddenly cut off near the end of the talk and directly after the following paragraph.

> If the leader understands his function differently from that thus established, if the leader does not repeatedly provide the led with clear details on the *limited nature* of the task and on

---

7. A few examples chosen at random may be helpful here. Each is taken from the 1545 edition, which is the basis of critical editions of the Luther Bible: Revelation 22:11 in *DBWE 6*, 136 and *DBW 6*, 127; Jeremiah 45:4-5 in *DBWE 8*, 150 and *DBW 8*, 152; Colossians 1:20 in *DBWE 15*, 367 and *DBW 15*, 352; Judges 6:15–16, 7:2, 8:23 in *DBWE 12*, 461 and *DBW 12*, 447–448.

8. In a lecture to his congregation in Barcelona, Bonhoeffer drew extensively on Bernhard Duhm's *Israels Propheten*, even using Duhm's translation of the Hebrew text throughout the lecture. *DBWE 10*, 325–341 and *DBW 10*, 286–302. Later in volume 10, we find Bonhoeffer alluding to Luther's translation without fully quoting it when he referred to 1 Corinthians 12:26 in an examination paper in July 1930. The text reads 'if one member suffers, all suffer together with it' (NRSV) or 'wenn ein Glied leidet, so leiden alle Glieder mit . . .' (Luther Bible), whereas Bonhoeffer left out the word member/*Glieder*: 'leidet einer, so leiden alle mit.' *DBWE 10*, 388 and *DBW 10*, 356.

9. Bonhoeffer, *DBWE 12*, 268–282.

their own responsibility, if the leader tries to become the idol the led are looking for—something the led always hope from their leader—then the image of the leader shifts to one of a misleader . . .[10]

On 30 January, two days before the address, Hitler had been named chancellor. Though Bonhoeffer had been preparing the talk before 30 January and he never used Hitler's name, no one could have misunderstood who Bonhoeffer had in view. What is in doubt is the reason the broadcast was ended so abruptly. Bethge described the situation this way:

> . . . . Bonhoeffer's microphone had been switched off. Was it merely because he had overrun his time? Can it be assumed that Goebbels's people had gained complete control of the station in the course of barely two days? Who found the conclusion of this broadcast so insufferable that he intervened? The script shows that the syllables had been carefully counted and worked out. Whatever the truth of the matter, it is significant that Bonhoeffer's remarks were cut off at the crucial point. With his talk deprived of its stinging conclusion, Bonhoeffer was very upset by the thought that he might actually be suspected of joining in the general acclaim.[11]

Unlike Bethge, however, Bonhoeffer scholarship has not necessarily seen much significance in the disruption of the lecture's transmission. The event is often called 'mysterious' and the like, simply narrated without comment, or it is claimed that Bonhoeffer merely went over his time limit.[12] John Moses notes that the Nazis did not begin moni-

---

10. Bonhoeffer, *DBWE 12*, 280.
11. Eberhard Bethge, *Dietrich Bonhoeffer: A Biography*, revised edition, edited by Victoria J. Barnett (Minneapolis: Fortress, 2000), 260.
12. For example, Robert Koch uses the word 'mysterious,' Ruth Zerner simply says that the concluding paragraph 'never aired,' and Christiane Tietz tells us in her excellent biography that Bonhoeffer had merely exceeded his allotted time. Robert F. Koch, 'The Theological Responses of Karl Barth and Dietrich Bonhoeffer to Church-State Relations in Germany, 1933–1945,' (PhD, Northwestern University, 1988), 131; Ruth Zerner, 'Dietrich Bonhoeffer's Views on the State and History,' in *A Bonhoeffer Legacy: Essays in Understanding*, edited by AJ Klassen, (Grand Rapids: Eerdmans, 1981), 141; Christiane Tietz, *Theologian of Resistance: The Life and Thought of Dietrich Bonhoeffer*, translated by Victoria J Barnett (Minneapolis: Fortress, 2016), 36.

toring radio broadcasts until 25 March, and one might presume that if there were isolated exceptions before then, the effort would not have been made for a relatively little-known theology lecturer.[13] Ferdinand Schlingensiepen had little to add about the event other than a footnote explaining that the German word for 'misleader,' the final word Bonhoeffer uttered before his mic was cut, is *Verführer* (a play on words with *Führer*), 'which in its more usual sense means "seducer."'[14] Charles Marsh goes somewhat further, writing, 'Bonhoeffer would begin speaking of Hitler as the Antichrist', but offers no commentary on this statement or explanation tying that claim to the radio broadcast.[15] Very little beyond this is typically asserted about the end of the broadcast, perhaps because scholars assume the motives of those who turned off the microphone are lost to history.

There may be more to the story, however. By using the word *Verführer*, Bonhoeffer may have been calling Hitler the Antichrist in a fairly direct manner. The typical word for Antichrist in German is simply *Antichrist*, and in modern translations 1 John employs this word; Luther uses a similar word, *Widerchrist*. However, in addition to meaning 'seducer' or 'deceiver,' the word *Verführer* is also closely associated with the idea of Antichrist, especially in 2 John 7. Here is Luther's version juxtaposed with the English New Revised Standard Version:

> Denn viele Verführer sind in die Welt gekommon, die nicht bekennen Jesum Christum, daß er in das Fleisch gekommen ist. Das ist der Verführer und der Widerchrist.
> Many deceivers have gone out into the world who do not confess that Jesus Christ has come in the flesh; any such person is the deceiver and the antichrist!

In the few passages in the New Testament outside 1 John that might be thought to involve the Antichrist (or an antichrist), Luther almost always employs a form of *Verführer*. The noun form, *Verführung*, appears in 2 Thessalonians 2:9–12 in the passage about the so-called

13. John A Moses, *The Reluctant Revolutionary: Dietrich Bonhoeffer's Collison with Prusso-German History* (New York: Berghahn, 2009), 104.

14. Ferdinand Schlingensiepen, *Dietrich Bonhoeffer 1906–1945: Martyr, Thinker, Man of Resistance*, translated by Isabel Best (London: T&T Clark, 2012), 388.

15. Charles Marsh, *Strange Glory: A Life of Dietrich Bonhoeffer*, (New York: Knopf, 2014), 160.

Man of Lawlessness. Then in Revelation the Beast and the False Prophet (19:20) and the Devil himself (20:10) are said to *verführen* humanity.[16] Even if Bonhoeffer had not meant to call Hitler the Antichrist, one can see how those in the control booth may have misunderstood.

Of course, this does not prove that Bonhoeffer's address was cut short because he called Hitler the Antichrist. Perhaps he really did simply run out of time. That the mic was cut immediately after the word *Verführer*, however, would seem to make that possibility much less likely. It seems probable that Bonhoeffer did indeed claim that Hitler was an—or even *the*—Antichrist, and his microphone was probably cut by those running the studio either because they themselves were offended or because of the fear of what might happen to them if the transmission continued.

'Stations on the Way to Freedom'

One further example of Bonhoeffer's use of Scripture will suffice to make my point about the usefulness of keeping the Luther Bible by our sides. In the second stanza of his poem 'Stations on the Way to Freedom,' we find Bonhoeffer considering 'Action,' which is the title of the stanza below.

> Not always doing and daring what's random, but seeking the right thing,
>
> Hover not over the possible, but boldly reach for the real.
>
> Not in escaping to thought, in action alone is found freedom.
>
> Dare to quit anxious faltering and enter the storm of events,
>
> Carried alone by your faith and by God's good commandments,
>
> Then true freedom will come and embrace your spirit, rejoicing.[17]

---

16. An older spelling, *verfüret*, is used here in the 1545 edition. One might also take note of Genesis 3:13 when Eve says that the serpent deceived her. While Luther used '*betrog*' (cheated), later translations have preferred *verführen*.
17. Bonhoeffer, *DBWE 8*, 513.

Barry Harvey has pointed out for English language Bonhoeffer readers that the verb 'ergreifen,' translated in the second line as 'reach,' might be better rendered as to seize or grasp. Because 'the nature of reality, as Bonhoeffer understands it, is grounded in God's becoming human in Jesus Christ', Harvey writes, '... taking hold of the real gives fitting expression not only to his theology but to the course his life took up to the very end.'[18]

This phrase becomes all the more striking when one realizes that Bonhoeffer may be making an allusion here to Paul's letter to the Philippians. Consider Luther's translation of Philippians 3:10–14 alongside the NRSV, which employs 'obtained' and 'make it my own' where Luther uses 'ergreifen.'

> ... zu erkennen ihn und die Kraft seiner Auferstehung und die Gemeinschaft seiner Leiden, daß ich seinem Tode ähnlich werde, damit ich gelange zur Auferstehung der Toten. Nicht, daß ich's schon ergriffen habe oder schon vollkommen sei; ich jage ihm aber nach, ob ich's auch ergreifen möchte, nachdem ich von Christo Jesu ergriffen bin.

> I want to know Christ and the power of his resurrection and the sharing of his sufferings by becoming like him in his death, if somehow I may attain the resurrection from the dead. Not that I have already obtained this or have already reached the goal, but I press on to make it my own, because Christ Jesus has made me his own.

The reader will recall that immediately after these sentences Paul employs a famous metaphor that compares his life in Christ to a race in which, 'forgetting what lies behind and straining forward to what lies ahead' (v 13), he presses on toward the 'goal' of God's call. Bonhoeffer appears to have something similar in mind in the stanza entitled 'Action.' If this sounds odd, remember that for the Bonhoeffer of *Ethics*,

> *reality* is first and last not something impersonal, but *the Real One*, namely, the God who became human. Everything that exists receives from *the* Real One, whose name is Jesus

---

18. Barry Harvey, *Taking Hold of the Real: Dietrich Bonhoeffer and the Profound Worldliness of Christianity* (Eugene, Oregon: Cascade, 2015), ix.

> Christ, both its ultimate foundation and its ultimate negation,
> its justification and its ultimate contradiction, its ultimate Yes
> and its ultimate No. Trying to understand reality without the
> Real One means living in an abstraction, which those who live
> responsibly must always avoid.[19]

If this is so, then Paul could have affirmed Bonhoeffer's entering 'the storm of events' and avoiding abstraction because by 'taking hold of the real' Bonhoeffer meant exactly what Paul had in mind in Philippians 3: taking hold of Jesus Christ.

Obvious rebuttals to this claim might spring to the reader's mind. Bonhoeffer is clearly allowed to employ *ergreifen*, even multiple times, without referring to Philippians 3. It is also possible that the allusion, if it was an allusion, was entirely unintentional. But we should keep in mind that Bonhoeffer had been working on *Ethics*, the book which he hoped would be his magnum opus, until his arrest, and he continued thinking about it in prison.[20] Paul was also in prison when he wrote Philippians.

There are further, more intriguing parallels. During the dark hours in Tegel he spent working on this poem, Bonhoeffer thought of death, but he did so with hope and perhaps even pleasure. In the final stanza of the poem, he called death the 'highest of feasts' when he would finally discern freedom 'in the countenance of God.'[21] This seems similar to the way Paul understood death; earlier in the letter he had told the Philippians it would be 'far better' for him to die and be with Christ (1:23). It was, he told them, his 'desire.'

There was one major difference between the two men's situations, of course. Paul sensed that his time on earth was not yet spent (1:24–25). The churches still needed him, and God would not take him just yet. Bonhoeffer, however, finished this poem more than a month after the attempted coup of July 20, 1944, and he appears to have been coming to terms with the thought that there was only one way he could leave prison a free man. He would only be free by shuf-

---

19. Bonhoeffer, *DBWE 6*, 261–62.
20. As Bonhoeffer wrote to Bethge on December 15, 1943, 'I have the feeling that I am becoming significantly older here and sometimes think my life is more or less behind me and all I have left to do is to complete my *Ethics*.' Bonhoeffer, *DBWE 8*, 222.
21. Bonhoeffer, *DBWE 8*, 514.

fling off this mortal coil. For this reason, he began the final stanza of 'Stations on the Way to Freedom,' a stanza simply entitled 'Death,' by addressing death itself with a striking imperative: 'Come now, highest of feasts.'[22] Bonhoeffer could face death in this way because he had run a race like the one Paul had run two millennia before, a race in which they strove for the same goal.

Conclusion

Paul is not the only biblical figure with whom we find Bonhoeffer comparing himself during his two years in Tegel prison. Around the same time Bonhoeffer wrote a longer poem entitled 'The Death of Moses' in which God says to Moses, "You shall glimpse salvation from afar, / but your foot shall not itself cross o'er!'"[23] Concerned about the reconstruction of Germany and the German church after the war, Bonhoeffer may have felt himself to be in a similar position. Bonhoeffer's hope was like Moses's: 'Through death's veil you let me see at least/ this, my people, go to highest feast.'[24] A poem called 'Jonah' too is written about this time; perhaps Bonhoeffer himself felt cast away in the bowels of Tegel Prison as Jonah had been cast overboard by the sailors.[25]

These lines of thought came naturally to Bonhoeffer only because the intellectual waters he swam in were biblical through and through. For that reason, Anglophone readers would do well to pay closer attention to Bonhoeffer's reading of Scripture and especially to the Luther Bible. Certainly, the German language changed significantly between Luther's day and Bonhoeffer's, and often, as in the two cases above, no matter how much digging we do, some ambiguity about Bonhoeffer's intentions will remain. That is inevitable. Yet it is also undoubtedly true that reading the Luther Bible alongside Bonhoeffer's works will continue to unearth other important details or allusions that have so far gone unnoticed.

---

22. Bonhoeffer, *DBWE 8*, 514.
23. Bonhoeffer, *DBWE 8*, 532. The background is Moses's conversation with God and death on Mount Nebo. See Exodus 34.
24. Bonhoeffer, *DBWE 8*, 540. Note the use of 'highest of feasts,' also used in 'Stations of the Way to Freedom.'
25. Bonhoeffer, *DBWE 8*, 547–548.

Bearing the Impossible Present: Bonhoeffer, Illegality, and the Witness for Migrants

Myles Werntz

Introduction

In the twenty-first century, the question of immigration continues to vex both theological and political thinking. As a more sustained phenomenon of contemporary social existence, immigration is an inescapable facet of how nations are constituted, and a generative question to which national actors, as well as Christians within those spaces must continue to return. Globally, migration continues to pose challenges unseen since the Second World War. Even prior to the outbreak of the COVID-19 virus, which has prompted closure of borders on every continent, migration populations had increased by over 100 million in the last twenty years.[1] This increased migra-tion, though not the exclusive cause of a new wave of populism, has resulted in a bevy of calls to rethink the role of the nation-state in ways which minimize the role of migration in political life.[2] Within my own context, approximately fifteen million persons live undocu-mented in the United States, for both economic and political reasons, persons whose lives and livelihoods are intertwined with American neighborhoods and localities. The tensions of migration have been

---

1. https://www.un.org/en/development/desa/population/migration/publications/migrationreport/docs/InternationalMigration2019_Report.pdf. The United Nations report, though one of the best available aggregated data collections, accounts for less than fifty self-reporting nations, making the actual number of migrants much higher than the reported numbers.
2. For a survey of these policies particularly in North America and Europe, see *Crimmigrant Nations: Resurgent Nationalism and the Closing of Borders,* edited by Robert Koulish and Maartje van der Woude (New York: Fordham University Press, 2020).

accentuated with the passing of the IIRIRA in 1996, in which mil-
lions of undocumented persons whose lives were fully grounded in
the United States became caught in this conflict between law and
common practice.[3]

Background

In this article, I will draw upon Bonhoeffer's 'Lecture on the Path of
the Young Illegal Theologians of the Confessing Church' for wisdom
as to how to negotiate the interstice between contemporary law surrounding immigration and future aspirations regarding the law. I will
do so by first sketching how contemporary theorists negotiate this
interstice between present law and future aspiration.

Following this, I will turn to Bonhoeffer's lectures to the ordinands,
not to make an analogy between the illegality of the ordinands and
the illegality of migrants, but to show that there are certain structural
features of the ordinands' vocation which Bonhoeffer offers in these
lectures to his listeners that will help them to endure their status. These
features, I contend, offer a vision for how churches might embody
theological hope for migrants. Being able to connect migration to
Bonhoeffer does not occur in a straightforward fashion, as would happen in, for example, discussions of Scriptural exegesis or theological
anthropology; one cannot, for Bonhoeffer, simply apply a Scriptural
injunction in a straightforward way to public policy, for this is to con-
fuse church and world. As I will restate shortly, Bonhoeffer is not interested in policy for the sake of policy, but, as a pastor and theologian,
what it means for the churches to bear witness and to be the body of
Christ in the world. Policy is thus only describable as an outworking of
a theological ontology; the people of God can act in the world for the
world only as they are first the people of God. As immigration policy
is an evolving field what is needed here is not a final policy, but rather
wisdom on how—as Christian theologians and practitioners—to bear
the space between present and future for the presently undocumented.

The operative assumptions of this essay are three-fold. First, migration is an enduring feature of creaturely life, and thus unavoidable

---

3. For background, see Christiana Gerken, *Model Immigrants and Undesirable
   Aliens: The Cost of Immigration Reform in the 1990s* (Minneapolis: University of
   Minneapolis Press, 2013).

for any political entity to have to address.[4] Secondly, migration has always functioned in practice in ways which exceed current juridical features of the law. I make no argument here for the moral necessity of the practice of migration as such, beyond that which is intrinsic to the flourishing of human persons; insofar as politics serves the common good of human creatures, no law will encapsulate the manifold exceptions necessary to attend to the reality of migration. Accordingly, in contemporary immigration theory—both as posed by the ongoing refugee crisis and by the more sustained patterns of immigration which continue to constitute the existence of nation-states—there is a gap between that which is legal and that which is an aspirational hope for many who migrate outside established channels. This gap creates an unresolvable surd for those whose flourishing is caught between the present realities and future hope. Without disputing the need for preventing illicit rationales for migration—namely, those forms of migration entangled with harm to humans—these is likewise, a perduring need for an account of how one is to hope for a better legal framework with which to aid licit migration, including family reunification, economic need, and humanitarian aid.

It is this gap between the legal and the aspirational which hangs over much of Bonhoeffer's later writings, particularly as it pertains to a future which is able to more properly attend to the cultivation of human life. Bonhoeffer's own history is one interlaced with migrations to America, England, and Spain, but it is not there that I believe he provides guidance on the question of immigration. With so many excellent recent resources for thinking theologically about immigration now, why Bonhoeffer?[5] Particularly in an age of globalization,

---

4. For the phenomenological features of this claim, see Thomas Nail, *The Figure of the Migrant* (Stanford: Stanford University Press, 2015).

5. Some of the best recent theological resources for approaching immigration (leaving to the side sources focused on the Scriptural, practical, and moral dimensions) include Rob Heimburger, *God and the Illegal Alien: United States Immigration Law and a Theology of Politics* (Cambridge: Cambridge University Press, 2018), Elaine Padilla and Peter C. Phan, eds., *Contemporary Issues of Migration and Theology* (New York: Palgrave Macmillan, 2013), Gemma Cruz, *Toward a Theology of Migration: Social Justice and Religious Experience* (New York: Palgrave Macmillan, 2014), and Tisha M Rajendra, *Migrants and Citizens: Justice and Responsibility in the Ethics of Immigration* (Grand Rapids: Eerdmans, 2017). Of these, Heimburger's dogmatic and historic approach, as opposed to arguments rooted in political theory of rights, liberationist impulses, or postcolonial theory, is closest to the approach of this paper.

why does a theology of migration need insights from a European theologian?

In offering this reading from Bonhoeffer, this is not to displace the insights from scholars who speak to immigration out of their own advocacy; Bonhoeffer, though an immigrant to Spain, England, and America, never draws these experiences into his own theological reflections. What Bonhoeffer does offer, however, is a different and reorienting kind of gift. Rather than offer Christian wisdom for immigration rooted in his own biography and identity, Bonhoeffer's ecclesiology offers an account of what it means to be the body of Christ in the world, bodies who are able to bear the distance between the present law and the future hope. In excavating Bonhoeffer's wisdom for ordinands who find themselves caught between law and custom, we will find not only political wisdom, but ecclesial and pastoral insight for Christian participation in contemporary immigration struggles globally.

Immigration in Contemporary Perspective: The Question of Belonging and Law

In a variety of ways, contemporary theorizing of immigration turns on a duality of law and immigration practice, attempting to negotiate a way through the present moment in which the laws of the land remain in force as organizing social structures. In her essays on the interrelationship between citizenship, nationality, and land, Saskia Sassen has unpacked the tension between contemporary nation-states, which rely upon bounded territories, and global economic and political arrangements which call territorial notions of citizenship into question. Sassen argues not only do these globalised arrangements make it difficult to name who is responsible for economic and politically-motivated migrations, but these globalized situations undermine our notions of what counts as 'belonging' to a place. In contrast to territorialized nations, global movements ranging from international recognition of human rights, to digital relationships and relational networks upset a territorially-rooted understanding of who 'belongs' in and to a nation.[6] Even if we count 'belonging'

---

6. Saskia Sassen, *Territory, Authority, Rights: From Medieval to Global Assemblages* (Princeton: Princeton University Press, 2008), 278–280.

under the rubric of those who pay taxes—thinking by this measure to exclude undocumented immigrants or other non-citizens from our definition—the innumerable taxes which are paid by non-citizens (and not paid by citizens) gives us a fuzzy situation in which laws of citizenship do not comport to the lived realities of those in a place.

What Sassen trades in her proposal is territory for de-territorialization—a world of independent states for a world in which territory and citizenship follows the flows of human capital. This border-less solution to immigration is a common conclusion from other directions as well. Seyla Benhabib's proposal for transnational citizenship likewise trades on moderns as transnational beings whose identity is not circumscribed by territories, but by their linkages in digital spaces, global exchange, and post-territorial understanding of identity.[7] Other post-Marxist approaches, such as Sandro Mezzadra and Brett Neilson, and Michael Hardt and Antonio Negri, which emphasise the unity of the 'commons' across borders dispute the nature of territorial belonging, but see the work of those like Sassen as too wedded to neoliberal economic assumptions.[8] The anthropological and philosophical work of Thomas Nail likewise presents a genealogical argument for borders as not following a reified people, but rather those entities which produce personhood; put differently, for Nail, all of nature is in a state of transfer—whether water, soil, or persons, which technologies of various kinds—such as dams, gardening, and borders—are attempting to subvert and stabilize.[9] A free flow of persons is quite simply the practice of nature, and whether we theorize this transnational flow according to digitalization, 'the commons', or capital is beside the point.

Theologically, these insights find their exemplars in liberationist accounts of migration. In Jorg Reiger's proposal, Christian notions

---

7. Seyla Benhabib, *The Rights of Others: Aliens, Residents, and Citizens* (Cambridge: Cambridge University Press, 2004).

8. Sandro Mezzadra and Brett Neilson, *Border as Method, or the Multiplication of Labor* (Durham: Duke University Press, 2013); Michael Hardt and Antonio Negri, *Multitude* (Cambridge MA: Belknap, 2005) and *Commonwealth* (Cambridge MA: Belknap, 2011). See also, Riva Kastoryano, 'Transnational Nationalism: Redefining Nation and Territory', in *Identities, Affiliations, and Allegiances*, edited by Seyla Benhabib, Ian Shaprio, and Danilo Petranovic (Cambridge MA: Cambridge University Press, 2007).

9. Thomas Nail, *The Figure of the Migrant* (Stanford: Stanford University Press, 2016).

of travel find their reworking in the person of Jesus, the mendicant Word-made-flesh, such that 'those of us who have the privilege to travel under less pressure have a choice to make . . . to stay connected with the common people.'[10] Migration for economic or political reasons is not dissimilar from leisure travel for Reiger, but we bias our perspective toward the travel which occurs to spend money as opposed to that which is done to acquire capital. In a different way, Illsup Ahn's claim that God is 'distinctly yet intrinsically involved with the phenomenon of human migration within God's grand vision of liberation and redemption'.[11] In both cases, the theological resolution of migration questions rests on reading the life of God into the life of migrants as such, for in migration, we find mirrored the true ontology of human life: freedom, or in this case, the capacity for free movement.

If these proposals immanentize a future world for undocumented migrants through recourse to extra-legal bases, putting forth a vision of what could or should be if we were to conceptualize 'belonging' under a different rubric than that of territorial law, other proposals, such as Mark Amstutz's recent book accept territorial sovereignty as the realist framework within which our thinking concerning immigration must fit.[12] Following in wake of Reinhold Niebhur, Amstutz's proposal is a realist communitarian proposal which describes national identity as requiring circumscribed borders, in contrast the aforementioned proposals. Given that all nations operate with certain entrance and visa requirements, the question of immigration must resolve in terms of the existing legal frameworks. For Amstutz, deferring to law is a moral judgment, writing that 'the rule of law is not an ancillary attribute of representative government; rather it is the *moral* foundation of legitimate governmental rule based on consent'.[13] Amstutz's designation of law as the *moral* foundation of a people is significant, in that it denotes the inviolability of a legal framework

---

10. Joerg Reiger, *Faith on the Road: A Short Theology of Travel and Justice* (Downers Grove, IL: IVP Academic Books, 2015), 36.
11. Illsup Ahn, *Migration and Theology* (Leiden: Brill, 2019), 28. See in particular his link between the Holy Spirit's sanctification of creation with the movement of migrants, 67–81.
12. Mark R Amstutz, *Just Immigration: American Policy in Christian Perspective* (Grand Rapids: Eerdmans, 2017).
13. Amstutz, *Just Immigration*, 41, emphasis added.

for more than pragmatic reasons. Citing multiple Scriptural examples in which nations are authorized by God to implement moral law, Amstutz's work defers to civic law as the framework within which we negotiate the good of persons, regardless of common practice.[14] The divergence between these two positions leaves us at an impasse between law and practice, that one must either immanentize the future without respect for present law, or work within current law, but without a clear sense of how to moral address the multiplicities of contemporary migration practice which fall outside the present law. Amstutz is not alone here in adopting this position, but represents broadly a position which sees law as an enduring feature of human community, without which there can be little possibility for sustaining social existence.[15] Amstutz maintains that moderated migration is essential for polities, but also that absent the framework of law, there can be no communities for migrants to be assimilated into.

In both sets of proposals, what is missing is an account of the interstitial, a transitional theological account which would assist in overcoming this divide between legal frameworks on the one hand, and the extra-legal practice which corresponds to the practices of migration. For both frameworks assume some kind of legal code to regulate practice, but what is left out in both instances is an account of transition beyond one legal framework and into another, where practice must operate in a space of illegality.

Before turning to Bonhoeffer's contribution to this question, we must recall that for Bonhoeffer, it is not of primary concern of theology to provide proper social policy, insofar as the church is not the totality of the nation, nor is the goal of theology to provide political formulations which can be adopted without remainder by a nation. Rather, it is the purpose of theology to bear faithful witness to the work of God in Christ, and to build up the body of the church which operates within the economy of creation. It is in this way that theology then serves the nation, as an angular and indirect witness to proper

---

14. Amstutz, *Just Immigration*, 216.
15. Others following this position include James K Hoffmeier, *The Immigration Crisis: Immigrants, Aliens, and the Bible* (Wheaton: Crossway, 2009), Matthew Soerens and Jenny Hwang Yang, *Welcoming the Stranger: Justice, Compassion and Truth in the Immigration Debate* (Downers Grove, IL: IVP Books, 2009), and Peter Meileander, *Toward a Theory of Immigration* (New York: Palgrave Macmillian, 2001).

policy, by bearing witness to the truth of created reality, the substrata to which political policy must be accountable.[16] As we move toward Bonhoeffer then, political insight is not generated by articulating first principles, but by reflecting on the primary ground of theological reality: the manifested reality of Christ in the church.[17] When reflecting upon a complex social reality such as migration, then, to follow Bonhoeffer's lead, what is needed is not a political theory which seeks simply ameliatory counsel from the church, but chastened political thought which follows from the form of confession of the church. This bears certain resemblances to the methodology envisioned by the liberationists above, with one important modification: the experience from which theological wisdom proceeds is not unalloyed, even if it is the experience of those who suffer. Rather, the wisdom of human experience must be refracted through Christology, through which we understand the grounds and ends of creation.

To briefly see how Bonhoeffer's own position diverges from both the forementioned approaches to the surd of migration, recall his comment in the *Ethics* that 'The divine mandates depend solely on God's one commandment as it revealed in Jesus Christ. They are implanted in the world from above as organizing structures—"orders"—of the reality of Christ, that is of the reality of Gods' love for the world and for human beings that has been revealed in Jesus

---

16. There is for Bonhoeffer a vantage point for political thought to which Christian confession provides an asymmetrical position. By being able to name its end properly, Bonhoeffer says, only the church can speak of its beginning and its middle, such that it is able to articulate an anthropology which then is fitting for political life to operate from. See Barry Harvey, 'The Narrow Path: Sociality, Ecclesiology, and the Polyphony of Life in the Thought of Dietrich Bonhoeffer', in *Being Human, Becoming Human: Dietrich Bonhoeffer and Social Thought*, edited Jens Zimmerman and Brian Gregor (Eugene, OR: Pickwick Publishers, 2010), 102–126.

17. Michael Mawson, *Christ Existing as Community: Bonhoeffer's Ecclesiology* (Oxford: Oxford University Press, 2018), 130–131. The church is not a *societas perfectas* but insofar as it bears witness to Christ, the ground and firstfruits of creation, is properly positioned to offer political insight. See Bonhoeffer, *Ethics*, DBWE 6:55: 'In Christ we are invited to participate in the reality of God and the reality of the world at the same time, the one not without the other. The reality of God is disclosed only as it places me completely into the reality of the world. But I find the reality of the world always already borne, accepted and reconciled in the reality of God.'

Christ.'[18] Reflecting his earlier judgments on the proper ordering of creation echoing back to his lectures on Genesis, and even to his first dissertation,[19] Bonhoeffer holds that the good order of creaturely life is that which proceeds from and follows the shape of Christian confession, but which is not identical to it, in the way that Adam is both being transformed by Christ while not being Christ. One cannot do away with the mandates of creation, which for Bonhoeffer includes governance, for these are part of creaturely life which sustain and order it, though they are being transformed by the work of Christ. In the time between, however, the body of Christ suffers the distance to bear witness to the Christic reality of creation.

In moving now to Bonhoeffer's lectures to the young ordinands, it is important to observe both what Bonhoeffer does and does not offer us. Bonhoeffer, as I have argued, is concerned with the shape of creaturely life, and particularly what sustains it, but he is not interested in it in a straightforward fashion. To put differently, even for straightforward injunctions from the Old Testament to care for migrants (for example, Leviticus 19:34) must pass through the church in order to be borne out into the world. It is to misunderstand the task of theology to make this kind of straightforward move, especially if it means flattening Scripture into a mode of ethics.[20]

It is to Bonhoeffer's lectures to the young illegal ordinands that we turn now to see what it means for the church to bear such a mark. For only if excavating what it means for the church to bear the distance between law and future hope can we begin to understand the basis upon which the church extends that hope into the world. Accordingly, we must now take out time understanding what Bonhoeffer means for the church to bear that distance by exploring his comments to a group of young ministers faced with just that conundrum.

---

18. Bonhoeffer, *DBWE* 6, 390.

19. Bonhoeffer's own development beyond the framework in the dissertations is due in no small part to his exposure to the Christological framing of the theological task by Karl Barth. But even here, Bonhoeffer writes that 'Because, however, the entire new humanity is established in reality in Jesus Christ, he represents the whole history of humanity in his historical life. Christ history is marked by the face that in it humanity-in-Adam is transformed into humanity-in-Christ', in *DBWE* 1, 147.

20. Here, consider Bonhoeffer's criticism of American Christianity as 'Protestantism without Reformation', in part for its conflation of Christianity as ethics. See 'Protestantism without Reformation', in *DBWE* 15:438–462.

The Confessing Church and the Possible Impossibility of Legal Vocation

In October 1938, Bonhoeffer gave a lecture on the path of the young illegal theologians of the confessing church to an extraordinary (as opposed to regularly scheduled) meeting of the Confessing Church Brethren in Pomerania. The Confessing Church's history in that particular region had been strong nearly to that point, as many of the ministers in training from the Confessing Church were in parishes in the area, and much of the training of the Confessing Church had taken place in the villages of Pomerania, such as Finkenwalde. In the months leading up to his October address, Bonhoeffer had written to the "young brothers" about the coming 'hour of severe temptation'.[21] By 1938, the initial fervor which the Pastors Emergency League had fueled had been dampened; in September of 1937, the school at Finkenwalde had been sealed, the Confessing Church had been excluded from forthcoming World Council of Churches discussions, and Himmler's Decree had opened up an avenue for Confessing Church ordinands to return to the Reichchurch. Conditions for the young ordinands was not helped by the fact that though the synods of the region were sympathetic to the Confessing Church, as Bethge describes it, the churches were content to remain Lutherans, and thus, moderate on the question of whether it was proper for the churches to resist the Reich both theologically and politically.[22]

In his January 1938 letter to the Pomeranian synod, Bonhoeffer implores the young pastors who are losing heart to remember that the storms are arising against them because Christ is in their boat;[23] bolstering their resolve was not simply a matter of inspiring them with words, but pointing them to the structures which would help facilitate their increasingly difficult, and now illegal, vocation. In this letter, he asks them where the organs are which bolster parish life, such as 'the district Councils of Brethren . . . which could help the district pastors bear their great responsibility' and 'the Pomerian confessional synod, which could only genuinely emerge through the congregation, and which should have shown the way for the Pomeranian church? In

---

21. Bonhoeffer, 'To The Young Brothers in Pomerania', *DBWE* 15, 29–36, (29).
22. Eberhard Bethge, *Dietrich Bonhoeffer: A Biography* (Minneapolis: Fortress Press, 2000), 432.
23. *DBWE* 15, 30.

other words: why did we in Pomerania not seriously implement the insights of the Dahlem synod?"[24]

The Dahlem Synod of 1934, which Bonhoeffer mentions here and elsewhere in his writings to the Pomeranian brothers, was a response to Barmen's call for theological fidelity, but in contrast to the bracing language of Barmen, appears rather prosaic in its concerns. As opposed to Barmen, which lays out the theological objections to the German Christian Church, Dahlem focuses on the *institutional* organs necessary to implement the theological vision of Barmen. In the synod declaration, the distinction between the Reich church and the true church appears along the line of the Reich Church's 'usurped autocracy' and 'legal administration' which has 'set up an impossible Papacy in the Evangelical Church'.[25] The remainder of Dahlem highlights similar structural infidelities, such as the elimination of synods, the binding of office-bearers of the church, leaving them with no choice but to create 'new organs of government', organised in accord with the Confessions.[26] Tellingly, Dahlem says that 'All the protests, warning and admonition which we have raised, taking our stand on Scripture and Confession, have been in vain. On the contrary, the Reich Church Government, appealing to the Fuhrer and using the getting co-operation of political forces, has continued ruthlessly its work of destroying the Church'.[27]

Put differently, where Dahlem sought to succeed was, in contrast to Barmen, by meeting the theological challenge of the Reich Church on the field of administration and organisation, for it was in this way that the ordinands could sustain their illegal vocation. The young pastors' illegal status was not with respect to the law of God—for their pursuit of vocation was ultimately one of Gospel against which there can be no law. Their illegality was due to their being at odds with the law which supported the organisational bodies essential to embody this theological struggle: confessions which must be made in congregations, congregations joined together in synods, and synods bound by their confessions of Scripture.

---

24. *DBWE* 15, 31–32.
25. 'Dahlem Declaration', in JF Maclear, *Church and State in the Modern World: A Documentary History*, 384.
26. Maclear, *Church and State in the Modern World*, 385.
27. Maclear, *Church and State in the Modern World*, 384–385.

By the time Bonhoeffer gives his October 1938 lecture to the young illegal theologians, theological education has continued beyond Finkenwalde, but in a far more tenuous space than three years earlier, when the Confessing Church's synodal and administrative organs were much stronger. Bonhoeffer offers them encouragement, repeating themes from an August 1938 letter to them, promising them the presence of Christ even in the midst of institutional collapse. While Barmen, he tells them, properly expresses the theological witness of Scripture, Dahlem is an 'exposition of the third and fourth theses of Barmen,'[28] which had 'accepted God's word as the commission to call for correct proclamation and to correct church order. This was not just a theoretical matter', he writes, 'but one that needed to be put into practice.'[29]

The six aspects of Dahlem which Bonhoeffer lays out in the remainder of his speech are the church's unity, leadership, a leadership which serves the gospel and arises from the church instead of the state,[30] proclamation which is tied to the church's existence, obedience to the true and not heretical church, and leaving the future organizational existence of such a church into the hands of God. All of these are practically wise, but the preoccupation with right order seems an odd message to give to ordinands discerning whether to stay with the Confessing Church or seek legalization, as right order is collapsing around them.

Bonhoeffer speaks to the illegal theologians about the need for institutional stability in their state of illegality, not as a pipe dream, but because it is through these institutions that their illegality can be sustained. This is the irony: that attending to the institutional features of synod, confession, and ordination, the illegal theologians might find the structural outworking of their confessions necessary to *sustain* their illegal status in the eyes of the state. For Bonhoeffer, this proper organization is not purely ordered toward times of self-preservation; prior to 1938, much of the Confessing Church's actions with respect to the government had been to show itself as a viable and legal alternative to the Reich Church. But by 1938, this vision of the Confessing Church as legally existing alongside the Reich Church had been put to rest.

---

28. *DBWE* 15, 421.
29. *DBWE* 15, 423.
30. *DBWE* 15, 423–424. The third point concerning the nature of church leadership included 'can only be called by the church itself', presumably in distinction from church organs being instituted by state offices.

In its refusal to reconcile with the German Christians, in creating parallel structures, and accepting its illegal status, 'Dahlem has acted on behalf of (*stellvertretend*) the entire church', he writes, arguing that the Confessing Church and its ministers are not embracing permanent illegality, but a presently legally guilty status for the sake of those who do not yet see their error.[31] Setting up parallel structures could be the road of schism and separation, but in remaining subject to the charge of illegality—an illegitimate charge from the Confessing Church's perspective—the Confessing Church has bound itself to the church universal, suffering for their error, and refusing to be a pure sect.[32] This theme, appearing across the corpus, has been said to appear in a more passive form (interceding, praying for the weakness of another) during this period, but this seems to be a more active notion of bearing guilt, appearing prior to the writing of Ethics; in building up a corporate framework which is a building out of the church's confession, the corporate church actively bears the judgment of the legal system for the sake of its calling, the ones it houses, and for the churches which remain in moral error.[33]

In their corporate obedience to Christ, the Pomeranian churches and their ordinands bear their illegal vocations together, mirroring the churches of Paul who bore with his own imprisonment.[34] Proper synodal leadership was essential to this task, for without it churches fell into schism from one another, or worse, church leadership would become concerned with maintaining an institution and not responding to God's own word through institutional means.[35] Ministers who commit themselves to their vocation as ministers of the Gospel should not worry about the legal guilt they incur, for ultimately, Bonhoeffer writes, guilt incurs not from their illegal status, but from not implementing Dahlem's vision in a full-throated sense, seeking instead the accomodationist vision of the German Christians.[36]

---

31. *DBWE* 15, 424.
32. *DBWE* 15, 425.
33. Jennifer McBride, *The Church for the World: A Theology of Public Witness* (Oxford: Oxford University Press, 2011), 13–14 has argued for the distinct senses of *stellvertretung* as divided between the era of pastoral ministry and the writing of *Ethics*. I am suggesting the active sense appears long prior to *Ethics*.
34. *DBWE* 15, 427.
35. *DBWE* 15, 430.
36. *DBWE* 15, 436.

Legal Church, Undocumented Members

I have explicated the institutional aspects that Bonhoeffer sees as necessary to sustain an illegal vocation, but in order to adequately draw these insights into the question of immigration, we may not simply apply the ecclesial claim to the political sphere, for the law of a peoples—responsive as it might be to the suasion of the Christian community—is not the object of Bonhoeffer's commendation here.

To move by analogy, we must move not into policy but into church disposition: for churches to sustain that which is envisioned as illegal by the law, it must be done in coordination with other churches, churches interested in fidelity to the call of Christ, leaving the survival of their labors to God. But to fully tie this together, we must draw in one unspoken piece of Bonhoeffer's argument in these lectures: that the basis of the church's *stellvertretung* for the world is on the basis of what Christ has done in the church.

Here, we must recall Bonhoeffer's ongoing writings regarding the status of the Jews within the Confessing Church. For Bonhoeffer, the Confessing Church struggle, including its struggle for a sustained and orderly church, was tied together with being able to survive as a church for the Jews, but not as an abstracted object of pity. From his first dissertation forward, Bonhoeffer had argued for the value of the Jewish roots of the Christian faith; he would later extend this value to Jews who had been included by baptism,[37] and finally, on the basis of these prior acts of God, to the protection of the Jews as a whole.[38] The purification of the German church by the state of all Jewish families and influence was a betrayal for Bonhoeffer not only of the state's role vis-à-vis the church, but a move which threatened to make the whole church apostate—how could one conceive of a church which was not intertwined with the Jews? Because God had already included the excluded of the state into the life of the church, the advocacy of the Jews as such was grounded in the prior witness of the church.

---

37. *DBWE* 12, 'The Church and the Jewish Question', 368: 'The church cannot allow the state to prescribe for it the way it treats its members. A Baptized Jew is a member of our church. For the church, the Jewish question is therefore different from what it is for the state.'

38. On this development, see Ruth Zerner, 'Church, State, and the "Jewish Question"', in *The Cambridge Companion to Dietrich Bonhoeffer*, edited by John W DeGruchy (Cambridge: Cambridge University Press, 1999), 190–206.

His concern for the institutional form of the church as a means for sustaining the illegal vocation of the ordinands was not, in other words, so that a renewed church could exist which would simply reify existing ethnic standards of German priority within the church, but that a new church in which there was no ethnic priority might be established. Again, this was not out of commitment to a political ideal, but out of fidelity to the prior work of the Spirit, which had included the Jews both as progenitors of the faith and in the act of baptism. In Bonhoeffer's view, to be asked to abandon the work of Christ on behalf of the church was not only to abandon the only basis upon which we can hope for the world's salvation, but it was to refuse to be the church. It was, as has been amply discussed by many, an issue of *status confessionis*, an issue pertaining not just to the church's faithful witness, but an issue pertaining to the church's proper confession regarding its origin and source.[39]

With this in view, we can now see where Bonhoeffer's work on the question of how to sustain illegality finds purchase on the question of aid to undocumented immigrants. If we assume that the question of Christian advocacy for immigration flows from church to immigration, we assume erroneously that immigration is something *external* to the church, forgetting that many undocumented migrants are baptized members of the body of Christ. In doing so, we fail to see that the challenge of illegal migration is one which is, by analogy, one which calls the churches to recall that members of their own global body are being deprived. In its more insidious form, treating immigration as an external issue for ecclesiology assumes an ethnocentric vision of church, in which one ethnicity or nationality is the home, and all others are alien presences. In drawing an analogy between the *status confessionis* accorded to the Jews and that advocacy which should be accorded for the undocumented, I am not proposing a transposition of Jews into modern day undocumented immigrants, but arguing that analogously, the presence of the undocumented as members of the body of Christ opens the necessity for the churches to witness on their behalf.

---

39. For a careful parsing of this term and its conditions for use, see Michael DeJonge, 'Bonhoeffer, *status confessionis*, and the Lutheran tradition', in *Stellenbosch Theological Journal*, 3 (2017): 41–60.

To put our skepticism aside for the moment, the question of whether churches *will* hold open this mode of illegal witness in this manner is different from exploring the conditions under which they will be *able* to do so. Bonhoeffer's shift away from the day-to-day practicalities of sustaining the Confessing Church *as* war broke out in 1939 keeps open the question, I think, of what Bonhoeffer would have done vis-à-vis the Confessing Church movement; if, in 1938, Bonhoeffer was indeed despairing so much for the future of the future of the institutional church, it seems odd that he would spend his address to the illegal ordinands on institutional concerns.

Conclusion

Bonhoeffer's lecture to the ordinands, deployed against the backdrop of increasing strictures which would pressure the ordinands into abandoning their confession, is instructive for contemporary Christian practice in a four-fold manner. These four aspects together, I argue, provide the basis for Christian practice to bear the distance between present law and future hope, without succumbing to utopian projection or debilitating realism.

First, if in fact the commitment to advocate for the undocumented is a Christian one, it is done from the prior acknowledgment that Christ's church is already comprised of undocumented members, moving from the action of God to our practice in the world. Apart from this prior commitment, we are invoking a kind of natural theology in which social commitments reread theological ones. This first movement forces an acknowledgment of the peregrination intrinsic to church confession: that it is made toward God on the basis of God's prior activity, in this case, by drawing in those who are not of our nation into the household of faith.

Second, following from the first, this advocacy is one which is done by incorporating those who are deemed external to the church into its practices and worship. In Bonhoeffer's case, the early inclusion of the Jews consisted of retaining those of Jewish heritage in their pastoral roles, meditating on the Hebrew Bible, intimates a transnational worship which is not of one *volk* but of many, transgressing borders as mere historical accidents and not ontological realities.

Third, such ecclesiological resistance is by necessity an ecumenical act. One of the more mundane, but significant aspects of the Confessing Church was the manner in which it sought recognition by both the

German government and international bodies such as the WCC as a legitimate body.[40] The broader resistance of the ordinands was possible due to the networking of various parishes in Pomerania and beyond which were interlinked by their confessions, synods, and ordination processes. In this sense, romanticizing the work of singular congregations reinforce habits of the sufficiency of autonomous congregations, and minimize the shared work of confession amongst congregations.

Fourth, and most controversially, the work of advocating for those threatened by the rule of law must be done by the creation of an alternate provision of order. This is the most persistent feature of both Bonhoeffer's lecture, and the backdrop of the Confessing Church's work vis-à-vis the government against which this lecture becomes intelligible. Rather than seeking an abolition of governance, the Confessing Church sought a form of order and ordination within its body which would demonstrate an alternate, humane form of order. With respect to immigration, this means, among other things, Christians being able to advocate for asylum for those who are here, expanding federal notions of asylum through legislative process, and sheltering those who are in need of it but who have not yet obtained it. This is close to what Seyla Benhabib has termed the "jurisgenerative process", by which alternate configurations of order are produced by populaces in the face of legal aporia; what is suggested here, however, is that this process is not one which is first legislative, but an ecumenical and ecclesial witness which can become a prod for legal process.[41]

Bearing the weight of the interstice between law and future hope was not for Bonhoeffer simply a matter of eschatological thinking, but bearing the suffering of others in its careful planning and present practice. Bearing this weight required both thinking ecumenically and structurally, and offers instruction for Christians seeking contemporary wisdom for advocating for those whose lives lie caught between border, law, and custom.

---

40. As Keith Clements has argued, this ecumenical commitment changed form over time, from an internal exercise which allowed the Confessing Church to briefly withstand ecclesiastical pressures to an external one which sought to leverage international pressure over against Germany. See Keith Clements, *Dietrich Bonhoeffer's Ecumenical Quest* (Geneva: WCC Publications, 2015).

41. Seyla Benhabib, *Another Cosmopolitanism* (Oxford: Oxford University Press, 2006), 49. Benhabib envisions this process not taking place according to national sovereign communities, however, but along the lines of trans-national *demos* which emerge in the exchange of nationalities (69ff.)

Vol 8 No 1/2020

Book Review
Biblical Literalism: A Gentile Heresy:
A Journey into a New Christianity through the Doorway
of Matthew's Gospel

By John Shelby Spong
(New York: HarperCollins, 2016)

ISBN 978-0-06-236231-5. (xxii + 394 pages)

Why does this book merit a review in *The Bonhoeffer Legacy*? The short answer is because both Bonhoeffer in his day and Spong in our time had become acutely conscious of the key importance of the Jewish roots of our Christian commitment, our beliefs and our liturgy. The life experience of both scholars with their historical-theological insights have proven to be path breaking, both ecumenically and for inter-faith dialogue, not to mention divisive internal church debate. In Bonhoeffer's case, as he recorded in his fragments on *Ethics,* the role of the Jews, with their belief in the one creator God in the history of the West, is absolutely crucial. The Holocaust, perpetrated by ideologically deluded Nazis, was the greatest crime in world history. It was the culmination of historic anti-Judaism in Europe going back to patristic times. It is a measure of Bonhoeffer's erudition, magnanimity of spirit and the courage of his convictions to have already in 1944–1945 accused his fellow church-members of being guilty of 'the deaths of the weakest and most defenceless brothers of Jesus Christ', namely the Jewish people. This, and much more about the guilt of the Church with regard to the 'Jewish Question', is to be found in the pages of his *Ethics.* Bonhoeffer stands out as witness filled with the Holy Spirit and armed with his historical acumen to see the misconceptions of the early Church towards Jews and what had gone wrong, particularly with his countrymen in the twentieth century. Instead of appreciating the Jews as the brothers and sisters of Jesus Christ, they wrongly and tragically focussed on the alleged historic 'guilt' of those who clamoured for the crucifixion of Jesus.

In Bonhoeffer's witness, therefore, the key problem was in the way one comprehended the role of the Jews in world history. This is the very same concern evinced by the American Episcopalian Bishop, John

Shelby Spong, in his numerous works that have investigated the Jewish roots of Christianity and how, in particular, the New Testament was produced. I remember lectures on the subject of some sixty years ago when we learned that the New Testament was embedded in the old and that the Old Testament was revealed in the New. Our lecturer was one Canon Alexander L Sharwood, Th L, MA (Oxon). He was an up-to-date scholar for his time and would have been classified as a 'Prayer Book Catholic'. He often warned sternly about fundamentalist illusions, calling them 'Bibliolatry'. Since then, however, the fundamentalists, led by such figures as Billy Graham, have become increasingly vocal, amassing a fervent but naïve following under the banner of *Biblical Literalism*.

The foolishness of fundamentalism and the way it is glibly championed by today's TV evangelists and the graduates of fundamentalist colleges has demonstrably damaged the credibility of the Christian cause. Atheist writers such as Christopher Hitchens or Richard Dawkins pan Christians for their mindlessness in relying on fundamentalist advocates who are demonstrably purveyors of a false logic. But Dawkins is at least aware of some vigorous Christian theologians who distance themselves from fundamentalism. For example, in *The God Delusion* (2006), Dawkins cites examples such as Dietrich Bonhoeffer, Richard Holloway and John Spong who have all passed severe judgments on fundamentalism. Indeed, Dawkins cites Spong's, *The Sins of Scripture* (2005), as an excellent example of a liberal bishop, 'whose beliefs are so advanced as to be almost unrecognizable to the majority of those who call themselves Christian' (237). Here, Dawkins has hit the nail on the head. Fundamentalists have a closed mind and simply dismiss any critique from 'liberals' as devil's work. *Biblical Literalism: A Gentile Heresy* certainly belongs in this category as far as the ultra evangelical advocates of biblical inerrancy are concerned.

Spong has spent his priestly-academic life in rescuing Christianity from fundamentalism. The present study stands as a monumental challenge to the 'biblical literalists' to revise their position. Sadly, though, judging by the fundamentalist reviewers to date, few will be inclined to do this. The majority will continue to believe what they want to believe. That is a peculiarity of all fundamentalists among theologians, as well as historians. They evince a depressing inability to *hinterfragen,* that is to investigate what lies behind an ideological position or any commonly accepted views. Spong's work is distinguished by his industry in uncovering the layers of the New Testament text. And the key to this endeavour is to recognise the essential

Jewish cultural and liturgical matrix out of which the Bible as a whole was produced.

For many of us, Spong's work will be an eye-opener, both refreshing and edifying, especially if we have not paid much attention before to the history of the Synagogue. The age old 'anti-Jewish bias has kept the Christian churches locked in an anti-Semitic, Gentile exile'. (3) One cannot understand the New Testament if one remains wilfully ignorant of Jewish cultural heritage. Spong's aim is to overcome this baleful ignorance by showing just how Jewish 'the Christian gospels are and just how much they reflect Jewish scriptures, Jewish history and Jewish patterns of worship. To read the gospels properly [. . .] requires a knowledge of Jewish culture, Jewish symbolism, Jewish icons and the tradition of Jewish story telling.' (3) In short, we Christians need to understand the 'midrash', that is the Jewish literature that interprets and elaborates on the biblical text that was in vogue from the fifth century, at the latest, through to the medieval era. Spong has made it his mission to investigate this literature and has been able to shed such new light on the meaning of the gospels. In what follows, Spong demolishes the flimsy scaffold from which fundamentalist preachers today have so aggressively, without any real understanding of the *Sitz im Leben,* proclaimed the 'true word of God'.

It is shown here, using the example of Matthew's gospel, to what extent it becomes more comprehensible if one appreciates that it is really the product of Synagogue preaching about the prophet, Jesus of Nazareth. Jesus' Sermon on the Mount was never uttered by Jesus; it is rather the imaginative creation of Matthew's understanding of Jesus as the new Moses. His gospel is, in short, a Jewish book and, as Spong observes, the Jewish reader world have read it properly (130). There are many more examples given by Spong that document the 'midrash' character of the gospel. Indeed, Matthew tried to tell the story of Jesus as a liturgical document and the creation of the synagogue. All this rings true. We have been given a work that opens a new, enlightened way to get behind the flat, literal text with which we are familiar. With our understanding thus sharpened, we are better equipped to gainsay the conservative literalists who are guilty of intellectual laziness. I believe Bonhoeffer would have approved of Spong's perspective.

John A Moses
St Mark's National Theological Centre, Canberra, Australia
Charles Sturt University

Vol 8 No 1/2020

Book Review
Dietrich Bonhoeffer, Theology, and Political Resistance

Lori Brandt Hale and W. David Hall (editors).
Lanham, MD: Lexington Books.

ISBN. 978-1-4985-9106-5 (216 pages)

The edited collection is introduced by Victoria J Barnett who dispels any doubt about the relevance of Bonhoeffer's theology to the political realm. His latter-day notion of 'this-worldliness of Christianity' is to be found implicitly in his dissertation, *Sanctorum Communio*. The proclamation of the gospel is not for its own sake but for the sake of the world. The church is not there for its own sake but to provide the space where Christians encounter Christ in the other. Being Christian entails entering into a state of responsibility. Each of Bonhoeffer's major theological works tease out an aspect of this state of responsibility for the world, for the other. Victoria Barnett concludes the introduction with the words, 'The diverse issues raised by the contributors to this volume, and the range of insights they draw from Bonhoeffer's work, illustrate Bonhoeffer's continued relevance for the realm of practised, political theology.'

The book is divided into three sections, namely, *Historical-Critical Interpretation*, *Critical-Constructive Engagement*, and *Constructive-Practical Application*. In the first section, Michael DeJonge expostulates on the church as an agent of resistance, Jens Zimmermann writes about Bonhoeffer in the context of the natural law tradition, David Hall reviews the political meditations of Carl Schmitt, Walter Benjamin and Bonhoeffer, and Robert Vosloo makes use of the discourses in *Status Confessionis* in reference to Apartheid South Africa. In the second section, Jennifer McBride and Thomas Fabisiak utilise Bonhoeffer in mounting a theological resource for dismantling mass incarceration, Lori Brandt Hale writes of Bonhoeffer's theology compelling interfaith action, Lisa Dahill questions whether Bonhoeffer's social location makes much of his work inaccessible to marginalised populations, Di Rayson seeks in Bonhoeffer a theological resource for an eco-ethic in the time of the Anthropocene, and Karen Guth uses Bonhoeffer to address the very specific issue of the Confederate Monuments Debate in the USA. In the third section, John Matthews reviews the ways in which his own reading of Bonhoeffer has shaped his ministry in terms of political responses, Paul Lutter goes to the heart of the role of church as its practical work for the world and others in between Sundays, and Jeffrey Pugh makes particular application of Bonhoeffer's theology in casting light on the events of Charlottesville in 2017.

As Victoria Barnett suggests, each of the contributions elaborates on the central purpose of the book in drawing out the ramifications of Bonhoeffer's theology for a range of practical, in many cases cutting-edge, issues in the political regime. As a whole, the book testifies to the common belief among Bonhoeffer scholars that many of his theological perspectives are both timeless and timely. At a time that sees threats to world order and the survivability of freedom, democracy, the preservation of human rights and social justice, tenets central to both Christianity and its progeny in modern Enlightenment civilization, Bonhoeffer's theology stands tall for its potential to shed light and insight that cuts to the heart of both the problem and the potential solution. Each of the contributions, along with the introduction, is highly readable not only for the theologically informed but for any intelligent reader interested in those issues that threaten our existence and discerning those resets of mind and heart with potential to move the world community to a better, more sustainable place. The editors have done well in their targeted theme and in the authors that they selected to make application of it to a range of crucial issues of today.

Terence J Lovat
The University of Newcastle, Australia

Contributors

Dr John Moses is an Australian historian, history educator and Anglican priest. He is currently professorial associate in the School of Theology, Charles Sturt University, Australia. Professor Moses has been a regular contributor to Australian and international Bonhoeffer conferences and associated gatherings. He is the author of *The Reluctant Revolutionary: Dietrich Bonhoeffer's Collision with Prusso-German History*, Berghahn Books, 2009.

Dr Peter Hooton is responsible for the Research Secretariat which undertakes work in public theology at the Australian Centre for Christianity and Culture on Charles Sturt University's Canberra campus. He is a former diplomat and the author of *Bonhoeffer's Religionless Christianity in Its Christological Context* (Lexington Books/Fortress Academic, 2020).

Dr Joel Looper is adjunct professor at Baylor University, Waco, Texas, USA. He completed his PhD in Bonhoeffer Studies at The University of Aberdeen, Scotland, UK. His forthcoming book with Baylor Press is titled, *A Protestantism Without Reformation: What Dietrich Bonhoeffer Saw in America.*

Dr Myles Werntz is Director of Baptist Studies and Associate Professor of Theology at Abilene Christian University, in Abilene, Texas, USA. He is the author of *Bodies of Peace: Ecclesiology, Nonviolence and Witness*, Fortress Press, 2014.

Dr Terence Lovat is Emeritus Professor, The University of Newcastle, Australia, Senior Research Fellow, University of Oxford, UK, and Conjoint Professor, University of Glasgow, UK. He presented his recent research intersecting Bonhoeffer's theology with elements of Islamic theology as a keynote lecture at the International Bonhoeffer Congress, Stellenbosch, South Africa, 2020.

CPSIA information can be obtained
at www.ICGtesting.com
Printed in the USA
JSHW032001300322
24361JS00006B/246